QUEER

A GRAPHIC HISTORY

Meg-John Barker

Julia Scheele

Published in the UK in 2016 by
Icon Books Ltd, Omnibus Business Centre,
39–41 North Road, London N7 9DP
email: info@iconbooks.com
www.iconbooks.com

Sold in the UK, Europe and Asia by
Faber & Faber Ltd, Bloomsbury House,
74–77 Great Russell Street,
London WC1B 3DA or their agents

Distributed in the UK, Europe and Asia by
Grantham Book Services
Trent Road, Grantham NG31 7XQ

Distributed in Australia and New Zealand by
Allen & Unwin Pty Ltd,
PO Box 8500, 83 Alexander Street,
Crows Nest, NSW 2065

Distributed in Canada by Publishers Group Canada,
76 Stafford Street, Unit 300, Toronto, Ontario M6J 2S1

Distributed in India by Penguin Books India,
7th Floor, Infinity Tower – C, DLF Cyber City,
Gurgaon 122002, Haryana

Distributed in South Africa by Jonathan Ball
Office B4, The District, 41 Sir Lowry Road, Woodstock 7925

Distributed in the USA by Publishers Group West,
1700 Fourth Street, Berkeley, CA 94710

ISBN: 978-178578-071-4

Text and illustrations copyright © 2016 Icon Books

Edited by Kiera Jamison

Printed by Clays Ltd, St Ives plc

HOW TO INTRODUCE QUEER THEORY

Writing an introduction to queer theory poses something of a challenge. Why? Here are some of the reasons:

*Author of *A Critical Introduction to Queer Theory* (2003). We'll introduce a number of key authors throughout this book; bear in mind that speech bubbles attributed to them shouldn't be read as direct quotes - they're often paraphrased to give a sense of each author's ideas, rather than their exact words.

WHO ARE YOU?

When we were putting this book together, we imagined it being helpful to these kinds of people.

MAKING THINGS PERFECTLY QUEER

Clearly, any introduction can only give you part of the picture, and can't possibly cover the whole complex, diverse, and ever-changing world of queer theory. This book aims to:

WHET YOUR APPETITE TO FIND OUT MORE (THERE'S A LIST OF ACCESSIBLE FURTHER RESOURCES AT THE END OF THE BOOK).

EXPLAIN HOW QUEER THEORY BECAME NECESSARY AS A WAY OF QUESTIONING POPULAR - PROBLEMATIC - ASSUMPTIONS ABOUT SEX, GENDER, AND IDENTITY.

INTRODUCE YOU TO SOME OF THE KEY QUEER THEORY IDEAS AND THINKERS - AS SIMPLY AS POSSIBLE - AS WELL AS TO SOME OF THE TENSIONS WITHIN QUEER THEORY, AND TO THE DIFFERENT DIRECTIONS THAT IT HAS TAKEN IN RECENT YEARS.

PULL OUT WHAT SEEMS MOST USEFUL FROM QUEER THEORY FOR OUR EVERYDAY LIVES, RELATIONSHIPS, AND COMMUNITIES.

THE IDEA IS TO INVITE YOU INTO QUEER THEORY AND TO ENCOURAGE YOU TO TRY THINKING QUEERLY.

WHERE WE'RE HEADED

Through the rest of this book we're going to:

1. Explore the various meanings of the word "queer".
2. Consider how wider Western culture came to understand sex and sexuality in the ways that it currently does, and how queer theory challenges this.
3. Introduce some of the scholars, writers, and activist movements which provided the foundations on which queer theory is built.
4. Explain some of the key concepts that queer theory initially put forward and where they came from.
5. Describe how queer theory has engaged with popular culture, biology, and sexology.
6. Cover some of the main criticisms of queer theory, and tensions within it, and how queer theorists have responded to these.
7. Outline some of the main directions queer theory has taken in recent years.
8. Suggest some ways in which you might think more queerly in your everyday life.

WHAT IS "QUEER"?

The word "queer" has had many different meanings in different times and places. It originally referred to strangeness or difference, and became a term of abuse. It has since been reclaimed as a positive word.

It can operate as an umbrella term for people outside of the heterosexual norm, or for people who challenge the LGBT (Lesbian, Gay, Bisexual, and Trans) "mainstream". It can also be a way of challenging norms around gender and sexuality through different ways of thinking or acting.

"QUEER" MEANING STRANGE

The original meaning of "queer", in 16th-century English-speaking countries, referred to something strange or illegitimate, as in "there's nowt as queer as folk" or being "in queer street", meaning someone having financial difficulties.

Using queer to mean odd, in the 19th century, social reformer and founder of the cooperative movement, Robert Owen, famously said to a colleague: "All the world is queer save thee and me, and even thou art a little queer."

Even in the early 20th century the word "queer" was still often used in this way, for example, in Arthur Conan Doyle's Sherlock Holmes stories. There's also the American phrase "queer as a three dollar bill", from a similar time, suggesting something odd and suspicious.

"QUEER" AS HATE SPEECH

The earliest recorded use of "queer" as a form of homophobic abuse is said to be an 1894 letter by John Sholto Douglas, the Marquess of Queensberry. He was the father of Alfred Douglas and famously accused Oscar Wilde of having an affair with his son.

"Queer" quickly became a derogatory term for same-sex sex, or for people with same-sex attractions, particularly "effeminate" or "camp" gay men.

Queer

"Queer" was also used as a more general insult to make things questionable by associating them with same-sex attraction, in much the same way that the phrase "that's so gay" has more recently been used to imply that something is rubbish.

RECLAIMING "QUEER"

One activist strategy for dealing with racism, sexism, homophobia, and other forms of oppression has been for people to reclaim the very words that are used against them. Examples include the reclaiming of words like "nigger", "slut", "dyke", and "faggot".

In the 1980s, people in LGBT communities began to reclaim the word "queer" as either a neutral word to describe themselves, or as a positive form of self-identity. One early example was the activist group Queer Nation who circulated a "Queers Read This" flyer at the 1990 New York Pride march.

Nowadays this neutral, or positive, use of "queer" has found its way into mainstream culture with TV shows such as *Queer as Folk* or *Queer Eye for the Straight Guy.* "Queer" here is usually synonymous with "gay men" and sometimes still suggests that they might be good at stereotypically "feminine" things.

QUEER UMBRELLA?

"Queer" is also often used as an umbrella term for anyone who is not *heterosexual* (attracted to the "opposite" sex) or *cisgender* (remaining in the gender that they were assigned at birth). It's a snappier and more encompassing word than the ever-extending LGBTTQQIA, etc. alphabet soup.

However … there are problems with this usage for many older people who have painful memories of "queer" being hurled at them as a term of abuse. Also many queer activists take issue with it because, for them, queer is about those who are further outside of "normal". Queer theorists take issue with "queer" being used as an identity term.

QUEERER UMBRELLA?

Many queer activists see "queer" as an umbrella term for folk who are outside of the mainstream: both the heterosexual/cisgender mainstream and the conventional LG(BT)* mainstream.

They point out that being "equal" is not always "equally good" and question the gay rights movement's focus on things like marriage, consumer culture, and serving in the military.

Maybe the focus should also be on the groups under the queer umbrella who are *most* marginalized, such as those who are at everyday risk of violence, suicide, poverty, and homelessness.

* B and T are in brackets here because LGBT rights agendas are often driven by gay men and, to a lesser extent, lesbians.

QUEERING QUEER

Both queer umbrellas still risk maintaining a binary division between those who are seen as queer, and those who aren't. This division is also often based on people's *identities*.

Queer *theory* is all about breaking down these kinds of binaries, which oversimplify the world into everything being either *this* or *that*. So, it would question any understanding that has some people under the umbrella and some people outside of it.

Queer theory is also all about questioning identity, so it would challenge any kind of fixed identity categories of lesbian, gay, bisexual, asexual, etc., including queer if it's used in that way. Don't worry if you don't quite get these points, we'll be coming back to them.

MULTIPLE MEANINGS OF QUEER

It'll be helpful to try to hold all of these multiple – and sometimes contradictory – meanings of queer that we've just covered in mind.

"QUEER" CAN BE A(N):

NOUN: "A BUNCH OF QUEERS"

ADJECTIVE: "THE QUEER COMMUNITY" "MY RELATIONSHIP IS PRETTY QUEER"

VERB: "TO QUEER SOMETHING"

Queer theory generally sees "queer" as a verb. Queer is something that we do, rather than something that we are (or are not).

WE QUEER THINGS WHEN WE RESIST "REGIMES OF THE NORMAL": THE "NORMATIVE" IDEALS OF ASPIRING TO BE NORMAL IN IDENTITY, BEHAVIOUR, APPEARANCE, RELATIONSHIPS, ETC.

Michael Warner, author of
The Trouble With Normal (1999)

QUEER INTERVENTIONS

Three related – but slightly different – queer disciplines or interventions are mentioned throughout the book.

- Queer activism is a form of *sexuality/gender activism* that opposes assimilationist agendas of trying to show how "normal" LG(BT) people are. Instead it celebrates difference and diversity, and challenges things like the commercialism of the gay scene.

- Queer studies is an *academic discipline* that tries to move beyond lesbian and gay studies to incorporate other sexualities and to take a more critical approach to sexuality as a whole, including heterosexuality. This is similar to how a lot of women's studies departments became gender studies departments because masculinities and other genders are also important areas of study. It's *multidisciplinary* because it draws upon many other disciplines, e.g. sociology, geography, history, literature, cultural studies, media studies.

- Queer theory is a *theoretical approach* that goes beyond queer studies to question the categories and assumptions on which current popular and academic understandings are based.

15

WHAT QUEER HAS IN COMMON: ANTI-IDENTITY POLITICS

Queer activism, queer studies, and queer theory generally share an opposition to *identity politics*: the idea of fighting for rights on the basis of identity (e.g. as an LGB or T person). They might argue that it's always problematic to *fix* yourself – or others – as a certain kind of person, even if rights are gained on this basis. Fixing can lead to people feeling inflexible and unable to change, or being seen as only one part of themselves and not all that they are.

There's much overlap between queer activism, studies, and theory. All three are also plural: there are really multiple queer activisms, queer studies, and queer theories, which have different focuses, and which may contradict each other.

HOW WE CAME TO THINK THIS WAY ABOUT SEX: A (VERY) POTTED HISTORY

One key point of queer theory is that our understandings of sex, gender, identity (and pretty much everything) are *contextual*. That means they have all been understood, and practised, in very different ways over time and across cultures.

So it's important to start with a brief overview of how our understandings came to be as they are now. Here we'll focus on sexuality. We'll come back to gender and identity later.

UNDERSTANDINGS ARE ALWAYS CONTEXTUAL

Importantly, queer theory does not see our current view as the "correct" one – as if there were a constant march of progress resulting in better and truer understandings over time, and led by Western culture.

Rather our current understanding is just one possibility among many. Consider solo sex, for example. In the 19th century, "onanism" was seen as causing all kinds of physical and psychological problems. There were devices available to prevent people from masturbating.

Now solo sex might actually be prescribed by sex therapists in order to improve people's sex lives, but it's still not viewed as "proper" sex. When linked to online pornography, it's often regarded as a dangerous addiction.

THE EARLY SEXOLOGISTS

Sexologists such as Richard von Krafft-Ebing, Magnus Hirschfeld, and Henry Havelock Ellis began a project of categorizing and classifying sexuality around the end of the 19th century. They employed methods that were popular in the medical and scientific literature of the time.

So, it was not just that you were attracted to tall women and enjoyed oral sex best, but rather that your attractions and sexual preferences made you a certain *kind* of person. Previously sexual behaviours – such as sodomy – had been regarded as a sin or a crime, but not as making you a certain type of person.

Terms for many sexual identities emerged from these writings. This is why queer theorists sometimes talk about the "invention" of homosexuality (and heterosexuality).

OPEN AND CLOSED DOORS:
EARLY SEXOLOGICAL UNDERSTANDINGS

Early sexology opened the door to discrimination, criminalization, and pathologization (seeing people as wrong, bad, or sick) on the basis of their sexual identity.

However, it also opened the door to fighting for sexuality/gender rights on the basis of being a certain kind of person. Indeed, some of these sexologists were involved in the earliest versions of the gay rights movement.

There was also an emphasis in early sexology on dividing sex into normal and abnormal kinds: a project that lingers till this day. Early sexology cemented the idea that there are good and bad kinds of sex, not just a diverse range of possible practices and attractions.

FREUD

Sigmund Freud, the founder of psychoanalysis, was, of course, a huge influence on sexology. Like the early sexologists, many of his ideas have found their way into everyday understandings of sex.

> I POPULARIZED THE IDEA THAT THE MAIN PURPOSE OF SEX WAS PLEASURE RATHER THAN PROCREATION. BEFORE ME, SEX WAS GENERALLY ASSUMED TO BE PATHOLOGICAL UNLESS IT WAS PROCREATIVE.

Freud also introduced the idea of sexuality as something that develops, rather than being present in the brain from birth. However, he retained the idea of individuals reaching a stable sexual *object choice*: attraction to the "same" or "opposite" sex based on going through the Oedipus complex.

OPEN AND CLOSED DOORS: FREUD'S THEORIES

Freud's pleasure principle opened up the possibility that it might be okay to want sex for the pleasure of the act itself. However, his ideas of the mature sexual *aim* were also part of the reason that penis-in-vagina (PIV) sex became the gold standard against which people tend to measure all other sexual practices.

Freud's stage model of sexual development opened up the idea that sexuality isn't necessarily fixed from birth. However, it still suggested strongly that certain sexual attractions were less mature or healthy than others.

Although Freud himself advocated against "therapeutic" attempts to make a person heterosexual, the psychoanalysts who immediately followed him left a terrible legacy of viewing homosexuality as a sickness and trying to "cure" it.

MASTERS AND JOHNSON AND SEX THERAPY

William Masters and Virginia Johnson could be seen as the founders of sex therapy in its current form. In the 1950s and 60s, they conducted laboratory studies on the physiology of the human sexual response. They observed hundreds of participants taking part in more than 10,000 sexual acts under laboratory conditions, wired up to machines which measured their physiology (heart rate, lubrication, blood pressure, penile and vaginal size changes).

On the basis of this, Masters and Johnson came up with their "human sexual response cycle":

- Excitement (breathing, heart rate, and blood pressure increase)
- Plateau (muscle tension and circulation increase further)
- Orgasm (quick cycles of muscle contraction in the lower pelvic area)
- Resolution (muscles relax, blood pressure drops, and body slows down).

OPEN AND CLOSED DOORS:
EARLY SEX THERAPY

Masters and Johnson's research greatly improved understandings of what happens physiologically during sex, including the fact that most women need external clitoral stimulation in order to have an orgasm, and that clitoral and vaginal orgasms were physiologically identical. (Before that, the prevailing view had been Freud's: that vaginal orgasms were more mature and healthier.)

However, Masters and Johnson overwhelmingly studied heterosexual couples having penis-in-vagina intercourse, which concretized the view that that is what "real" sex is. They also still argued that women *should* be able to orgasm through PIV sex. Their sexual response cycle paved the way for the pathologization of sexual "dysfunctions" (low desire and lack of desire, lack of arousal, and difficulty orgasming).

GAY RIGHTS MOVEMENT

Also in the 1950s and 60s the *homophile movement* started in the US. This aimed to decriminalize homosexuality, to educate people about it, and to decrease homophobia. It generally used *assimilationist* strategies: arguing that homosexual people were the same as heterosexual people in all important ways, and fighting for equal human rights on this basis.

MATTACHINE SOCIETY

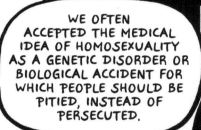

WE OFTEN ACCEPTED THE MEDICAL IDEA OF HOMOSEXUALITY AS A GENETIC DISORDER OR BIOLOGICAL ACCIDENT FOR WHICH PEOPLE SHOULD BE PITIED, INSTEAD OF PERSECUTED.

DAUGHTERS OF BILITIS

HOWEVER, WE ALSO CAMPAIGNED AGAINST THE COMMON BARBARIC "CURES" FOR HOMOSEXUALITY THAT WERE BEING USED AT THE TIME.

HARRY HAY

JAMES GRUBER

PHYLLIS LYON & DEL MARTIN

OPEN AND CLOSED DOORS: EARLY GAY RIGHTS MOVEMENTS

The homophile movement opened up the possibility of rights for LG(BT) people, and perhaps it fought for these rights in a way which was the least threatening to mainstream society – meaning that these arguments could be heard.

However, there are many problems with the kinds of assimilationist strategies it employed:

- They retain the status quo rather than pointing out the flaws in how mainstream society views sexuality, gender, etc.
- They perpetuate an *essentialist* model of sexuality: that it's a fixed aspect of identity.
- The "it's not our fault" idea easily slips into portraying homosexuality as inferior.
- By focusing on the acceptable face of white, middle-class, educated gay and lesbian people, they often maintain the oppression of those who do not fit that (the queerer umbrella).

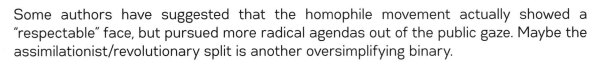

Some authors have suggested that the homophile movement actually showed a "respectable" face, but pursued more radical agendas out of the public gaze. Maybe the assimilationist/revolutionary split is another oversimplifying binary.

HOW WE THINK ABOUT SEX

These moments in history – and many others – have left us with the set of common understandings of sex and sexuality that we have now, embedded in the culture:

SEXUAL IDENTITY IS AN ASPECT OF WHO WE ARE THAT IS FIXED FROM BIRTH AND ENDURES THROUGHOUT OUR LIVES

SEXUALITY IS BINARY (STRAIGHT/GAY) AND BASED ON BINARY GENDER OF ATTRACTION (TO MEN/WOMEN)

PEOPLE CAN BE DIVIDED INTO NORMAL AND ABNORMAL ON THE BASIS OF THEIR SEXUAL ATTRACTIONS AND PRACTICES

Queer theory began by revealing all of these assumptions to be flawed, as well as showing how they helped to maintain a certain status quo.

KEY ASSUMPTION 1:
IDENTITIES ARE FIXED AND ESSENTIAL

This assumption can be questioned because of how *contextual* sexual identities and practices are: they're understood and experienced in very different ways at different points in time, and across different cultures and communities. Also, recent research has found that sexuality is *fluid*. Many people's experiences of their sexuality changes over the course of their lifetimes. Many adopt different identity terms at different times.

(ASSUMED) STRAIGHT GIRL

BUTCH LESBIAN YOUNG ADULT

SLIM GAY TEEN

BI BLOKE

QUEER BEAR

TRANS MAN IN RELATIONSHIP WITH A WOMAN

Queer theory goes beyond these points to challenge the whole notion of individual identity.

KEY ASSUMPTION 2:
SEXUALITY AND GENDER ARE BINARY

Neither sexuality nor gender is experienced as binary (clearly either/or) by everyone. When researchers ask people to place themselves on a continuum of sexual attraction, at least a third of people generally fall somewhere between "exclusively gay/lesbian" and "exclusively straight". More recent research from Tel-Aviv University has found that a similar proportion of people experience themselves to some extent as the "other" gender, as "both" genders, or as "neither".

1. TICK ONE:

FEMALE

MALE

BOTH/NEITHER

Queer theory goes even further than this in questioning the whole concepts of sexual and gender identity, and the links between the two.

KEY ASSUMPTION 3:
NORMAL AND ABNORMAL SEX CAN USEFULLY BE DISTINGUISHED

Historical shifts in which sexualities have been regarded as "normal" and "abnormal", and "functional" and "dysfunctional", bring the whole idea of distinguishing people on this basis into question.

We can also question what is meant by "normal". Many of the currently listed "paraphilias" (abnormal sexual desires) are very common, are practised by people consensually, and are associated with psychological well-being. So why regard them as abnormal? With major surveys finding that half of all people report having a sexual problem, is it normal to be "sexually dysfunctional"? Or does the very idea of sexual function create dysfunctions?

Queer theory goes beyond these questions to critique the "regimes of normativity" and "power relations" that such distinctions are based on.

ENTER QUEER THEORY

Queer theory, like the word "queer", is a much-contested term, always in flux, that is used in different ways by different academics and activists. This multiplicity and contradiction can be seen as a good thing by queer theorists who don't believe in simplistic explanations or universal truths anyway.

However, as we have seen, some unifying features of most queer theories could be:

- Resisting the categorization of people
- Challenging the idea of essential identities
- Questioning binaries like gay/straight, male/female

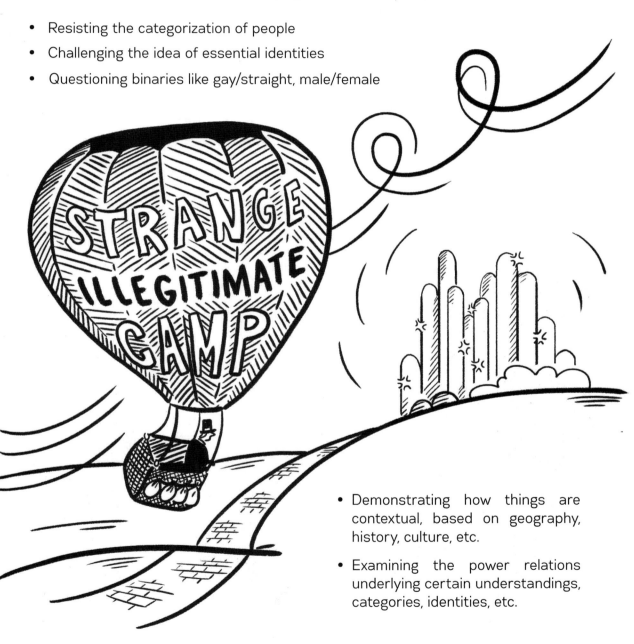

- Demonstrating how things are contextual, based on geography, history, culture, etc.
- Examining the power relations underlying certain understandings, categories, identities, etc.

Going back to "queer" as a verb, we might queer normative knowledge, identities, and institutions by showing how strange they are, by delegitimizing them, or by camping them up. This takes us right back to some of those original meanings of queer.

PRECURSORS TO QUEER THEORY

Of course, it's impossible to really put a starting point on queer theory, given that many of these ideas were around in some form or another before the term was coined.

Before we get into queer theory proper, let's touch on some of the important precursors to it during the mid-to-late 20th century. These are just a few of the thinkers who pre-dated queer theory, but who made similar points. Many of these ideas have been drawn upon – implicitly or explicitly – by queer theorists.

THE EXISTENTIALISTS

One important group of predecessors to queer theory in the early 20th century were the existentialists. Their central claim that "existence precedes essence" reverses the traditional essentialist assumption that humans have a fixed and fundamental essence which precedes the meanings that we give to ourselves, and to each other, through our experience.

For example, existentialists would question the idea that a person *is* an extrovert, or a coward, because they were born that way (*biological essentialism*), or because they became fixed that way through childhood experience (*social essentialism*).

SARTRE'S HOMOSEXUAL

For Jean-Paul Sartre, we're in "bad faith" if we deceive ourselves that we *have* to be a certain way (due to biology, or to social roles that are assigned to us, for example). Rather, we're in a constant process of self-creation, and are both free – and responsible – for what we create.

Controversially, another of Sartre's examples of bad faith was a "homosexual" who believed that his homosexuality was an inevitable and fundamental part of who he was. Queer theorists might agree with Sartre's critique of fixed and fundamental identities, but point out that he could equally have used a "heterosexual", or any other sexual identity, as his example here.

DE BEAUVOIR

Simone de Beauvoir emphasized the *limits* that are placed on our freedom to choose how to be. Sartre and de Beauvoir agree that the world that we are thrown into at birth already has many meanings present which constrain our freedom, but de Beauvoir more thoroughly examines the ways in which some people are freer than others. For example, the freedom to choose, of someone who experiences same-sex attraction, varies across different times in history, and different cultures.

ARISTOCRATIC WHITE MAN ←

WHITE MIDDLE-CLASS WOMAN →

WORKING-CLASS BLACK WOMAN →

BECOMING

De Beauvoir focuses – in *The Second Sex* (1949) – on gender. She clearly views our gender as something we become, rather than something fundamental that we are. However, she also highlights the huge societal pressures on women to deny their freedom and to focus on being "for-others" (the dainty girl, the desirable woman, or the nurturing wife and mother, for example), whereas men are generally more encouraged to embrace their freedom.

KINSEY: SEXUAL DIVERSITY

From a very different starting point to the existentialists, in the mid-20th century, US biologist Alfred Kinsey was another important precursor to queer theory. Kinsey was an early example of a *sex positive* researcher. His scientific studies of sexual behaviour were a response to the *sex negative* culture of the time, which had kept him and his students in ignorance about sex due to all the taboos surrounding it. He saw sex as benign and something people should be open about.

In addition to revealing that masturbation, sex outside marriage, and diverse sexual practices were far more common than were previously assumed, Kinsey also found that 37% of men and 13% of women had at least some overt same-gender experience to orgasm, and many more experienced some degree of same-gender attraction.

ONLY THE HUMAN MIND INVENTS CATEGORIES AND TRIES TO FORCE FACTS INTO SEPARATED PIGEONHOLES.

SEXUAL BEHAVIOUR OF THE HUMAN FEMALE

SEXUAL BEHAVIOUR OF THE HUMAN MALE

KINSEY: CATEGORIES ARE AN INVENTION

The famous Kinsey scale – used in these studies – opened up a new way of thinking about sexuality: as a spectrum between heterosexuality and homosexuality, rather than a binary. Sounding rather queer, Kinsey concluded that:

THE LIVING WORLD IS A CONTINUUM IN EACH AND EVERY ONE OF ITS ASPECTS. THE SOONER WE LEARN THIS CONCERNING HUMAN SEXUAL BEHAVIOUR, THE SOONER WE SHALL REACH A SOUND UNDERSTANDING OF THE REALITIES OF SEX.

Also there's a queer resonance in Kinsey's focus on what people did (behaviour) or experienced (attraction) rather than trying to classify them as certain types or fixed identities as the early sexologists had done.

But Kinsey's research failed to question another binary – that of gender. He produced volumes on the human "male" and "female", and sexuality is defined in terms of gender of attraction (same or opposite).

KINSEY'S LEGACY

Since Kinsey's time, scientific studies of sexuality have turned away from sexual diversity, generally concentrating on categories of sexual identity, often assuming these to be binary, and taking an essentialist view. Queer theory has remained distant from such research: ignoring or critiquing it. But perhaps the Kinsey studies help us to imagine an alternative science of sexuality that could (have) run alongside queer theory.

The prevalent notion from early sexology – that humans inhabit fixed sexual identities – was the lens through which Kinsey's findings were read by many gay activists.

SIMON AND GAGNON'S SEXUAL SCRIPTS

John Gagnon and William Simon worked at the Kinsey Institute and applied sociological ideas to sexuality in the 1960 and 70s. They questioned all the conventional ideas about sexuality being essential and were the first to suggest that the social world *produces* sexuality (rather than just shaping existing innate drives, as Freud suggested).

Simon and Gagnon's sexual script theory suggested that we constantly operate on three interrelated levels: cultural, interpersonal, and intrapsychic. We reflexively interpret material from our wider culture, and our interpersonal experience, through internal conversations with ourselves.

BEM'S ANDROGYNY

Around the same time as Simon and Gagnon's work on sexuality, psychologist Sandra Bem was challenging prevailing understandings of gender. Bem's research found that rigid adherence to masculine or feminine gender roles was not psychologically healthy – as had previously been assumed – and that it was actually better for people to be "androgynous", by which she meant being flexibly able to be "masculine" *and* "feminine".

Bem also studied how children internalize social gender roles, demonstrating that these are learnt rather than innate. She argued that gender was not a useful way of categorizing people and that we should move away from it. Later on she queerly said:

LET 1,000 CATEGORIES OF SEX/GENDER/DESIRE BLOOM. THROUGH THAT PROLIFERATION, WE CAN UNDO THE PRIVILEGED STATUS OF THE TWO-AND-ONLY-TWO CATEGORIES THAT ARE CURRENTLY TREATED AS NORMAL AND NATURAL.

BLACK FEMINISTS

In the 1960s and 70s, black feminist thinkers criticized both the civil rights movement (for neglecting gender) and the feminist movement (for neglecting race). They pointed out that different groups of women had very different experiences and agendas - that being a woman is not the defining feature of identity for those who also suffer other oppressions. For example, white middle-class feminist agendas are often alien - or even counter to - those of black and/or working-class women.

This undermined the assumption that there was any form of fixed, universal identity, as well as challenging any kind of identity-politics basis for activism. Instead, they focused on political and economic analyses of structures of domination. In this way, black feminist thought could be regarded as the root of both queer theory and queer activism.

MULTIPLE IDENTITIES AND MARGINALIZATION

Many black feminists laid the foundations of queer thinking around identities and marginalization.

In "Age, Race, Class, and Sex: Women Redefining Difference" (1984), black lesbian feminist Audre Lorde pointed out how unexamined privilege resulted in the category of "women" being taken to mean "white women" and black women being defined as "other".

bell hooks's writing also emphasizes openness about these differences and the importance of holding a position of resistance and compassion in activism.

RICH'S COMPULSORY HETEROSEXUALITY

The 1980s produced four landmarks on the way to queer theory, starting with Adrienne Rich's "Compulsory Heterosexuality and Lesbian Existence".

It's easy for academics and activists who critique normative ways of understanding sexuality to focus on *marginalized* sexualities, particularly LGBT sexualities. Rich turned the critical lens on heterosexuality, making the important queer point that we should examine *all* forms of sexuality, and how they operate in terms of social power – not just the non-normative ones. Rich argued that women are coerced into heterosexuality, and the associated patriarchal gender relations. This happens through the privileges and pleasures they gain from conformity with heterosexuality, and the punishments and losses associated with deviating from it.

(DE)CONSTRUCTING COMPULSORY HETEROSEXUALITY

Foreshadowing later queer theorists, Rich pointed out that all the effort that goes into enforcing compulsory heterosexuality reveals its very precariousness and instability. If heterosexuality was just natural, it wouldn't need to work so hard to shore itself up, and it wouldn't be so threatened by the alternatives to it.

THE DANGERS OF LESBIANISM: DARKNESS LONELINESS POVERTY

Rich's essay also introduced the idea of the "lesbian continuum" to capture all kinds of bonds between women (not just the sexual ones) as ways of resisting patriarchal compulsory heterosexuality.

BE AFRAID. BE VERY AFRAID.

Rich has been criticized for suggesting that all man–woman relationships are coercive, and that all woman–woman ones are political (not to mention keeping those gender binaries in place). She also failed to consider how compulsory heterosexuality oppresses gay men and other marginalized sexualities.

WITTIG'S STRAIGHT MIND

In "The Straight Mind", Monique Wittig pointed out that relationships between men and women were "obligatory" and that the institution of heterosexuality was so embedded within wider culture that it was invisible. The "straight mind" captures how heterosexuality is woven into our very processes of speaking, feeling, and thinking (e.g. only non-heterosexuals ask themselves why they are the way they are).

Wittig argued that gender and sexuality are so intertwined that being a woman only makes sense in a heterosexual context; lesbians are therefore not women! She has been criticized for similar reasons to Rich, and for suggesting that there are only two political responses to the straight mind: total conformity or radical revolution. This is another binary that it's easy to fall into. Both Rich and Wittig could also be criticized for focusing only on the intersections between sexuality and gender.

CRENSHAW'S INTERSECTIONALITY

Building on black feminist ideas in "Demarginalizing the Intersection of Race and Sex", founding coordinator of critical race theory, Kimberlé Crenshaw, developed the concept of intersectionality to demonstrate that no one axis of oppression (race, gender, sexuality, class, etc.) can be regarded separately from all of the others.

Intersectionality highlights the complex interaction between identities and unequal power relations that structure our experience in diverse – often contradictory – ways. These categories cannot be ranked in a hierarchy. Nor do they operate in a simple additive manner: rather they inflect and infuse each other in complex ways. Also they take on different forms and nuances depending on the context.

RUBIN'S THINKING SEX

Gayle Rubin's hugely influential essay, "Thinking Sex", considered sexuality on multiple dimensions rather than focusing on gender of attraction. Rubin wrote this during the "sex wars" of the 1980s (which continue to this day) between "sex negative" and "sex positive" feminists.* As part of the latter camp, Rubin argued against the oppression of sex workers, sadomasochists, and trans people, along with gay and lesbian people. She suggested that six ideologies operate together to constrain us:

GAYLE RUBIN

1. SEXUAL ESSENTIALISM

2. SEX NEGATIVITY

3. THE EXCESSIVE IMPORTANCE PLACED ON SEXUAL BEHAVIOUR (COMPARED TO OTHER BEHAVIOURS LIKE OUR EATING HABITS, FOR EXAMPLE)

4. THE SEX HIERARCHY

5. THE DOMINO THEORY OF SEXUAL PERIL

6. THE LACK OF A CONCEPT OF BENIGN SEXUAL VARIATION

SEX POSITIVE VS SEX NEGATIVE

PORN CAUSES SEXUAL VIOLENCE

SM DAMAGES PEOPLE

We've already touched on the first three of these ideologies, so we'll just explain the latter three here.

* Yes, this is yet another problematic binary – well done for noticing it!

THE SEX HIERARCHY

Perhaps the most famous image from Rubin's paper is one where she illustrates the sex hierarchy that cultures, religions, laws, psychiatry, mass media, etc. enforce between acceptable and unacceptable sex. Of course, different groups draw the line in different places, and where the line is placed shifts over time. However, the underlying assumption that we can delineate good and bad sex remains.

THE DOMINO THEORY

People reinforce this line between acceptable and unacceptable sex, believing it to stand between order and chaos.

Rubin's work highlights the dangers inherent in assimilationist gay rights, and other assimilationist, movements. We can fight to get our group into the charmed circle, but other groups further down the line will continue to be marginalized, pathologized, and criminalized: often those who are already most oppressed. The whole concept of a sex hierarchy needs to be undone. In its place, like Kinsey, Rubin argues for "benign sexual variation".

GAY RIGHTS/QUEER ACTIVISM

Queer activism – which emerged in the 1990s – challenges assimilationist movements that simply re-draw the lines on the sex hierarchy. Let's look at the history leading up to this.

Gay rights had moved on from the early homophile movement. In 1969, police raided an LGBT venue, The Stonewall Inn in New York, leading to a set of demonstrations known as the Stonewall Riots. Activists fought for spaces where people could be open about their sexuality without fear of being arrested.

THE FIRST GAY PRIDE WAS A **RIOT**

Following Stonewall, gay liberationists located oppression in social systems, and their goal was to transform these. They emphasized pride over pity, choice over essentialism, and liberation over assimilation.

AFTER STONEWALL

However, the liberation model didn't last. It gave way to a model – based on the main ethnic minority rights model of the time – that presented gay and lesbian people as a distinctive minority and aimed to achieve rights and legal protections *within* the existing social order.

The movement became individualistic, with its focus on personal coming out and being true to your identity.

HIV/AIDS AND ACTIVISM

One major reason that queer activism emerged was as a response to the AIDS crisis of the 1980s, which led to the following shifts in emphasis:

- From sexual identities to (safer) sexual practices: what you do rather than what you are.
- From essential identities to identities based on affiliation (e.g. affiliations between different groups affected by AIDS, such as gay men, other men who have sex with men, sex workers, friends, family, etc.).
- Towards resistance to the homophobic representations of AIDS as a gay disease, from science, policies, healthcare, and media representation, which was escalating homophobia and costing the lives of those with AIDS.

This renewal of radical activism was the starting point for groups like ACT UP and Queer Nation.

QUEER AGENDAS

Queer activism challenged previous *identity-politics* gay activism, which regarded sexuality as an essential, inherent component of the self. Activists emphasized militant protest against, rather than assimilation into, current systems, often through visible and confrontational tactics, such as taking over public spaces or outing closeted public figures. They were making the point that public space was heterosexual space and that alternatives to dominant culture were required for queers.

Further examples of queer activism include:

- *Queeruption* (part of the queercore offshoot of punk): an anarchist movement opposed to the lack of diversity in mainstream gay culture and its embrace of consumerism.

- *Gay shame*: a radical alternative to the commercialism of mainstream Gay Prides with their corporate sponsorship, ticketed events, and celebrity focus.

Like queer activism, queer theory also moved to focus on practices, the operations of power, and inclusive issue-based coalitions rather than exclusive identity politics.

THE TURN TO POST-STRUCTURALISM

Queer theory has its theoretical basis in the academic turn to post-structuralism in the 1970s and 80s. Post-structuralism is based on the work of various critical theorists, such as Jacques Derrida, Jacques Lacan, and Michel Foucault, although not all of them accepted that term themselves.

Post-structuralists reject the idea of any single, universal, absolute "truth". They're critical of systems of thought that make claims to uncover truths, such as science and religion. They're also critical of theories based on *grand narratives* that attempt to explain all of human experience in terms of one specific *structure*, like the theories of Freud (the internal structure of the unconscious) or Marx (the social structure of the class system).

POST -STRUCTURALISM 101

Post-structuralists see knowledge as always *partial* and *contextual*. What we know is only ever part of the picture, and it's based on who, where, and when we are. Knowledge cannot be neutral or objective; it's contingent on systems of power, and it shapes the *power relations* between people. Remember how religious and scientific "knowledges" of "homosexuality" emerged at certain points in time, and shaped how those with same-gender attraction were treated at those times?

Following Derrida, post-structuralists often *deconstruct texts*. This means they analyse literary, artistic, media, or scientific texts in order to uncover which binary oppositions are being privileged (e.g. rational or emotional, man or woman, sane or mad). Post-structuralists also offer multiple, even contradictory, readings of texts, as there can be no single true meaning.

OCCUPYING OUR IDENTITY

What post-structuralism means for us on a personal level is that there's no single truth about who we are. We can always tell multiple stories about ourselves, and none of them is the truth.

So, we don't have any kind of fixed, stable identity that we *are*. Rather, certain identities – such as those related to gender, sexuality, race, or class – are culturally constituted through ideological and normative processes. We come to *occupy* these identities through our relationships with the world in which we reside (which offers us different identity possibilities in different times and places).

SUBJECTIVITY

The idea of subjectivity is helpful here. As critical social psychology professor Margaret Wetherall explains, it helps us explore how we take up and live those culturally available category memberships and social roles as *agents* (beings with the capacity to do things in a given situation). We do this differently in different contexts, relationships, and wider power structures, rather than occupying one stable identity at all times.

QUEER THEORY IS BORN

Although some scholars (notably Gloria Anzaldúa) were already using the term "queer theory", most writers regard the birth of queer theory as happening at Teresa de Lauretis's conference of that name at the University of California, Santa Cruz in 1990. De Lauretis is an influential professor who is very engaged in the questions of subjectivity we just mentioned.

The queer theory conference led to a special issue of the journal *Differences: A Journal of Feminist Cultural Studies* on "Queer Theory: Lesbian and Gay Sexualities". So, the early focus was very much on sexualities, but the conference also discussed greater inclusivity (of bi and trans, for example), turning away from identity politics towards acts and practices, and exploring the ways in which power operates in relation to sexuality.

DE LAURETIS

De Lauretis saw queer theory as doing the following things:

- Refusing heterosexuality as the standard on which all sexual formations are based.

- Insisting that sexual subjectivity is shaped – through race and gender – in multiple ways.

AGENDER
POLYSEXU

BUTCH
FEMME
QUEEN

BI NON-
MONOGAMOUS
QUEER

GENDER
FLUID
TOMBOY

GENDER
CREATIVE

PLUS-SIZE
POLYAMOROUS
PANSEXUAL

PUNK
FEMME
DYKE

QUEER
TRANS
HARD FEMME

- Through this, moving away from the singular understanding of lesbian and gay studies.

BOI

UNDEFINED

NON-
BINARY
TRANS

QUEER
TOMBOY

ANDROGYNOUS
QUEER
TOP

QUEER TODAY, GONE TOMORROW?

However, de Lauretis rejected the term "queer theory" three years after the conference, feeling that people weren't using it in the political or critical way that she'd intended. This kind of thing has happened many times in the history of queer theory, as some have endeavoured to fix it as something stable, and others have resisted such fixing.

Queer theory, like all of us, has no fixed identity and multiple – contradictory – origin stories, rather than any one linear narrative. Like us it's plural rather than singular, in flux rather than static.

KEY FEATURES

As multiple queer theories developed over the 1990s, they generally shared the following features:

DRAWING ON **POST-STRUCTURALIST** theories to examine POWER relations RELATING TO **SEX, SEXUALITY, & GENDER**

...THROUGH

Destabilizing the TAKEN-FOR-GRANTED DOMINANT understanding which assumes that heterosexuality is the NORMAL or NATURAL standard of sexuality, and CATEGORIZES people in RELATION TO THIS

BY ...

EXPOSING how sexual and GENDER IDENTITIES ARE

CONSTRUCTED through the available ways of thinking and being in DIFFERENT times & places

PERFORMED: something that we **DO** rather than something that we (essentially) **ARE**.

FOUCAULT AND BUTLER

The two thinkers who are most frequently drawn upon in queer theory are Michel Foucault and Judith Butler. In fact, you've come across many of their ideas already. They're both notorious for being hard to understand, so let's get to know the basics.

Foucault focused more on sexuality, and Butler more on gender, although both of their ideas can be usefully applied to both, and woven together.

In *The History of Sexuality*, Foucault was one of the key thinkers to explore sexuality historically and to propose that it was *produced* by certain forms of knowledge (religion, science, etc.), rather than there being any truth we could uncover. In *Gender Trouble* Butler demonstrated how the concepts of gender and sexuality are intrinsically linked, and emphasized the move from seeing them as fixed essential identities, to *acts* or things that we *do*.

MICHEL FOUCAULT

Michel Foucault was a French philosopher, critical theorist, and historian of ideas. He was born in 1926 and studied philosophy at the École Normale Supérieure. He worked for several years abroad before returning to France and publishing books about madness, the criminal justice system, the methods for studying history, and, eventually, sexuality.

Foucault had sex with men, and he experienced many problems related to the legal and social constraints around gay sexuality. As a left-wing activist, Foucault also campaigned for human rights across the areas he researched. He died of neurological problems compounded by HIV/AIDS in 1984.

DO NOT ASK WHO I AM, AND DO NOT ASK ME TO REMAIN THE SAME.

At least, that's one story we could tell about who Foucault was ...

THE PANOPTICON

Foucault used the idea of 18th-century philosopher Jeremy Bentham, of a *panopticon*, to explain how contemporary society operates.

The panopticon is a prison with a tower in the middle and cells all around an outer circle, such that a guard sat in the centre could, at any time, be looking into any one cell. Because of this, prisoners begin to monitor their own behaviour.

This idea has been linked to the high degree of surveillance that we now have in much of the world, meaning that we *could* actually – most of the time – be being watched or recorded.

SELF-MONITORING SOCIETY

Foucault, however, used the panopticon to illuminate the ways in which people in contemporary societies become so aware of the various critical gazes upon them that they end up self-monitoring their own actions through fear that they might not be acceptable to others. This has developed into a culture where everybody polices *themselves* through fear of punishment, ridicule, and disapproval.

People are encouraged to scrutinize and judge themselves at all times: to improve and work on themselves, and to present a positive and successful self to the world based on the messages they receive about what counts as "normal".

NEOLIBERAL CONSUMER CAPITALISM

Foucault's panopticon is related to current *consumer capitalism*, which tells us we're lacking and flawed as individuals, and need something to "correct" this. It's also related to current individualistic *neoliberal* politics, which locate problems – and their solutions – in individual responsibility rather than in wider social structures and collective action.

POWER

Foucault argued that power has shifted from the *sovereign power* of pre-industrial societies – where rulers had the power of life or death over their subjects – to *biopower*.

The shift to manufacturing industries meant that the success of the economy rested on the productivity of the workforce. Thus governments needed more day-to-day power over the *bodies* of individual workers to ensure that they were productive (hence "bio" meaning "bodies"). But governments actually had a *less* direct relationship with workers, with expanding, and increasingly urban, populations.

Biopower is therefore a more diffuse form of power: spread out through society like a network, rather than the linear relationship between ruler and subject. It's also more pervasive, because individuals come under surveillance from multiple directions at once.

BODIES AND NORMALITY

Foucault argued that this need for biopower (to govern the bodies of the citizens) explains the current emphasis in contemporary Western societies on: *bodily* discipline and achieving *normality*. For Foucault, it's this emphasis that led to the emergence of sexuality as an identity category.

The body, at the centre of a web of power relations, is measured and categorized in many different ways (gender, race, mental health, disability, age, appearance, etc.), of which sexuality is one category. We are painfully aware of the extent to which we are considered "normal" on each strand of this web and we self-monitor in relation to this, for example when we read our friends' posts on social media.

DOCILE - AND INSECURE - BODIES

This self-monitoring results in a docile population with a strong commitment to conformity. The economy benefits in two ways:

- High levels of productivity (generating profit for employers)
- High levels of purchasing (of products that trade on our insecurities).

However, we also get high levels of mental health problems, general unhappiness, and alienation. Plus, we get the kind of *identity politics* way of viewing sexuality that regards it as characteristic of a certain type of person, which we need to prove is "normal" in order to get cultural acceptance. This way of seeing things was *reified* (made to appear real) by the work of early sexologists.

I'M TRYING TO GAIN RIGHTS ON THE BASIS THAT I HAVE A FIXED IDENTITY THAT IS AS NORMAL AS ANYBODY ELSE'S...

...BUT I COULD BE ASKING: **HOW** WAS THIS IDENTITY PRODUCED AND **WHY** DO I BELIEVE IT'S IMPORTANT TO BE NORMAL?

DISCOURSES AND TECHNOLOGIES OF THE SELF

Foucault argued that various *discourses* incite us to produce *knowledge* about our sexuality, which maintains certain *power relations*. Discourses are sets of ideas about something – like sexuality – that are present in religions, medicine, law, science, therapy, or popular media, for example.

He saw a key role for the process of *confession* in this. These discourses have encouraged us to tell our sexual stories to an authority figure. These narratives come to feel like the *truth* of our sexuality. Actually they're a means of internalizing social norms.

Foucault called this internalization and attempt to portray a "normal" fixed identity: *technologies of the self*. He was interested in exploring alternative technologies of the self, which were not prescribed by universals/norms.

YOUR IMPURE THOUGHTS ARE SINFUL

I KNOW YOU SPEAK THE TRUTH. I HAVE INTERNALIZED THIS DISCOURSE AND SHALL REPENT. I WILL TRY TO BE MORE NORMAL.

RESEARCH

POWER RELATIONS

Foucault didn't believe power is all one way. When a discourse is produced, at the same time a potential reverse discourse is also produced. For example, the invention of the "homosexual" person made possible stronger negative social controls, but also opened up the possibility of the gay rights movement.

Foucault was criticized for his broad-brush approach to history (later historians have since made a more attentive analysis of some of the periods he covered); he was also criticized for Eurocentrism, and for a lack of attention to how these things are gendered.

JUDITH BUTLER

Judith Butler is an American philosopher, literary scholar, and gender theorist. She was born in 1956 and has taught at the University of California, Berkeley since the early 90s. She has published books on bodies, language, power, nationality, and war, but it's her earliest work on gender which is perhaps best known, and most influential in queer theory. She has also been a vocal activist on LGBT issues and the Israel–Palestine conflict.

While Butler is often seen as *creating* queer theory, she didn't initially see herself as part of it at all!

I REMEMBER SITTING NEXT TO SOMEONE AT A DINNER PARTY, AND HE SAID THAT HE WAS WORKING ON QUEER THEORY. AND I SAID: "WHAT'S QUEER THEORY?" HE LOOKED AT ME LIKE I WAS CRAZY, BECAUSE HE EVIDENTLY THOUGHT THAT I WAS A PART OF THIS THING CALLED QUEER THEORY...IT CERTAINLY NEVER OCCURRED TO ME THAT I WAS...

YOU'RE WORKING ON QUEER THEORY? WHAT'S THAT?

??

At least, that's *one* story we could tell about Butler ...

THE CATEGORY OF WOMAN

The starting point for Butler's *Gender Trouble* (1990) was the problem of treating "women" as a unified coherent group. Both mainstream culture and feminism have tended to agree that "women" is a category which makes sense: whether that justifies stereotyping and discriminating against women, or fighting for rights and equality for women. Butler built on the previous criticisms of black feminists who pointed out that being a woman is not the defining feature of identity for those who also suffer other oppressions.

WHAT BUTLER SAW

Butler went beyond the criticisms of early black feminists to argue that, in reinforcing the idea of "women" as a stable, unified identity, feminism risked reifying and cementing the very gender relations that support inequality and oppression.

Everyone – including feminists – should avoid making generalizations and universal assumptions about "women" or "men" as if those were coherent categories.

THE ASSUMPTIONS OF IDENTITY POLITICS

You'll see similarities between Butler's ideas and the criticisms of the gay rights movement that we covered earlier:

- Rights based on one identity often slip into focusing on the agendas of the most privileged in that group (often white, middle-class people) and excluding/alienating others.
- More fundamentally, rights based on any kind of essential fixed identity risk undermining what they're fighting for, because they retain the binary (straight/gay, man/woman), the power relations underlying it, and the assumption that such categories make any kind of sense.

THE HETEROSEXUAL MATRIX

Media professor David Gauntlett nicely summarizes Butler's model – the heterosexual matrix – like this. This diagram shows how we tend to understand sex and gender, through wider cultural discourses.

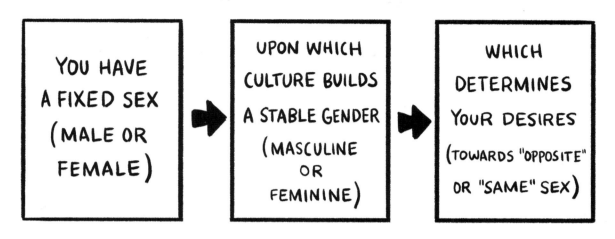

But Butler says we shouldn't accept that any of these follows from the last. Our bodies don't determine our genders, and neither do our genders determine our desires.

CHALLENGING THE HETEROSEXUAL MATRIX

Also, look how all of the words change between the heterosexual matrix and Butler's revised matrix:

GENDER PERFORMATIVITY

So, if gender is not simply a natural, essential, stable identity that we have because of having a male/female body – what is it?

Butler argues that it is *performative* – our gender *is* our expressions and behaviours (rather than those expressions and behaviours being the result of some underlying gender identity). Like sexuality, gender is what you *do*, not who you *are*.

Consider a day in your life and how you do your gender across different situations and relationships. Or over the course of your life (childhood, adolescence, adulthood, imagined future), how have you done gender at different times? This helps us see it's not a stable, fixed identity.

DOING GENDER

We operate within strong cultural discourses of what it is to be "a man" or "a woman" (which are produced by, and produce, certain power relations). We take these on and repeat them over and over so they feel very "real", as if these discourses were who we actually are. And in repeating them we also sustain the gender norms.

Performativity doesn't mean performance like an actor who could *choose* to perform in any way. We're limited in how we can perform by what is intelligible within the current gender system.

Vitally, there's no real, authentic performance of gender. *All* gender is imitative performance. A drag queen's performance that looks similar to the normative model of femininity is not a copy of an original, but rather a copy of a copy.

GENDER TROUBLE

If gender and sexuality are constructed *within* existing power relations, then there cannot be any gender or sexuality before, outside, or beyond these: no "authentic" gender or sexuality to compare others against.

Butler was clear that we can never step outside the existing power relations and discourses completely. We have to repeat gender performance on an everyday basis. However, we can do something different in *how* we repeat. We can create *gender trouble* and subversive confusion through parody, or other performances of gender, which challenge expectations. For example, through our daily performances of gender we can reveal how gender is constructed, or call binary understandings of gender into question.

You might be left wondering where "biological sex" and trans experience fit in with all this. We'll come back to this soon.

FOUCAULT AND BUTLER RECAP

Bringing the work of Foucault and Butler together, we can see that sexuality and gender are both socially constructed in certain ways, within current power relations. Specifically, sexuality and gender:

- Are both *seen* as an essential, fixed, vital part of our identity (who we are).
- Are intrinsically linked, because our sexuality is defined by our gender and the gender of who we are attracted to, and people often *read* sexuality off someone's gender expression (camp or butch, for example).
- Come to *feel* real, stable, and static through our internalizing of the available discourses, and repeated performance of them.

FOUCAULDIAN-BUTLERIAN RESISTANCE

Gender and sexual *constructs* can be resisted through:

- Recognizing that gender and sexuality are both multiple and fluid, and refusing to deploy *any* identity as a foundation because that would sustain normative structures.
- Questioning both binaries (male/female, straight/gay) and the links between them.
- Parody and subversive repetitions of diverse gender and sexuality performances – recognizing that sexuality can be about "bodies and pleasures" with no necessary connection to existing categories of gender and sexuality.

HETERONORMATIVITY

An extremely helpful concept in queer theory, which encapsulates a lot of what we've just covered is *heteronormativity*. Queer theorist Michael Warner popularized this term in 1991, drawing on Rubin's sex hierarchy and Rich's compulsory heterosexuality.

Heteronormativity refers to a set of related cultural assumptions:

- The "normal" or "natural" form of attraction and relationships is one man and one woman who:

    - Normally or naturally embody conventional gender roles and norms; and
    - Have sex whereby the man's penis penetrates the woman's vagina (PIV sex).

- Other forms of sexuality and gender are less normal or natural than this (or not normal or natural at all).

- Thus, people are assumed heterosexual unless proven otherwise.

HETERONORMATIVITY, HOMOPHOBIA, AND HETEROSEXISM

Heteronormativity is a different concept to its predecessors: homophobia, heterosexism, and straight privilege.

Homophobia generally refers to a negative set of attitudes towards gay and lesbian identified people and to "same-sex" sexual practices and relationships.

Heterosexism generally refers to bias or discrimination in favour of "opposite-sex" relationships and sexual attractions and in favour of heterosexual-identified people. Heterosexism helps us see that it's not just outright homophobia that's bad for LG people, but also things like having to decide whether to come out or remain closeted (both stressful), or having your sexuality assumed to be the totality of who you are, or the basis on which to question your masculinity/femininity.

...OH MY!

From a queer perspective, however, these concepts are problematic because they locate attitudes or biases within the *individual*. The idea of *institutional* or *structural* homophobia or heterosexism goes some way towards addressing this, but heteronormativity is helpful for locating the problem within cultural assumptions from the outset.

STRAIGHT PRIVILEGE

Straight privilege builds on the work of feminist and anti-racism activist Peggy McIntosh on *male privilege* and *white privilege*. McIntosh looks at how these privileges interlock to give straight white men advantages in life.

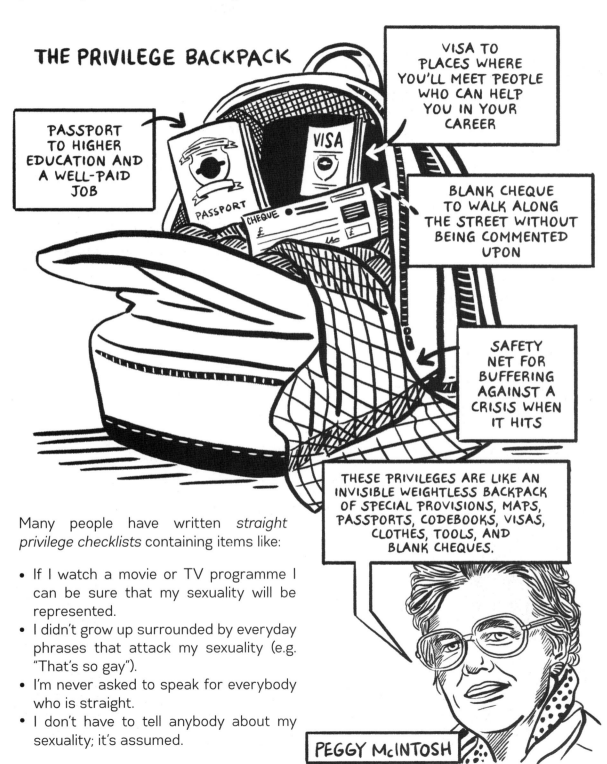

THE PRIVILEGE BACKPACK

PASSPORT TO HIGHER EDUCATION AND A WELL-PAID JOB

VISA TO PLACES WHERE YOU'LL MEET PEOPLE WHO CAN HELP YOU IN YOUR CAREER

BLANK CHEQUE TO WALK ALONG THE STREET WITHOUT BEING COMMENTED UPON

SAFETY NET FOR BUFFERING AGAINST A CRISIS WHEN IT HITS

THESE PRIVILEGES ARE LIKE AN INVISIBLE WEIGHTLESS BACKPACK OF SPECIAL PROVISIONS, MAPS, PASSPORTS, CODEBOOKS, VISAS, CLOTHES, TOOLS, AND BLANK CHEQUES.

PEGGY McINTOSH

Many people have written *straight privilege checklists* containing items like:

- If I watch a movie or TV programme I can be sure that my sexuality will be represented.
- I didn't grow up surrounded by everyday phrases that attack my sexuality (e.g. "That's so gay").
- I'm never asked to speak for everybody who is straight.
- I don't have to tell anybody about my sexuality; it's assumed.

PROBLEMS WITH PRIVILEGE

Having straight privilege is considered to be entirely positive, but one thing missing in the concept of straight privilege is the problems it poses for people on the *inside*, as well as those on the outside:

- The desperate fear that you might not be normal.
  If you have any fleeting same-sex attraction, find someone attractive who isn't your partner, or struggle with PIV sex.

- The strain of adhering rigidly to a set of masculine/feminine gender roles, and all the possibilities that closes down.
  Remember Bem's findings on gender rigidity.

- The difficulty of adhering to a set of standards that are also constantly changing.
  Such as the pressure to have adventurous sex whilst remaining inside heteronormativity.

- The guilt and shame of recognizing that your privilege is founded on the suffering of others and that you'll have to give some of it up in order to address that, or the inner conflict of trying to deny that this is the case.

OTHER NORMATIVITIES

One reason heteronormativity is a useful concept is that it doesn't say who it is good or bad for, but simply sets out the assumptions inherent in it. Also, unlike the other concepts we've just discussed, it's inclusive of many other normativities:

- *Monosexism*: people are normally or naturally attracted to only one gender
- *Sexual imperative*, or *compulsory sexuality*: people normally or naturally experience – and act upon – sexual attraction
- *Mononormativity*: the normal or natural way of relating is the monogamous couple
- *Cisnormativity*: people normally or naturally remain in the gender they were assigned at birth

From a queer perspective, it's not that any of these concepts (such as homophobia, heterosexism, straight privilege, and heteronormativity) is completely "right" or "wrong"; rather, they each open and close different possibilities.

INTERROGATING HETERONORMATIVITY

All of this means that we need to study heterosexuality – and other "normative" identities and practices – just as much as we do LGB sexualities and other "non-normative" ones. It's easy for queer theory to concentrate on LGBT people and more obviously "transgressive" practices, but, as sex critical professor Lisa Downing puts it:

THE DISCURSIVE TRAPPINGS OF HETEROSEXUAL RELATIONSHIPS, INTERCOURSE, AND REPRODUCTION DESERVE JUST AS MUCH CRITICAL SCRUTINY - IF NOT MORE, GIVEN THE HISTORICAL LACK OF ATTENTION ON WHAT IS PERCEIVED TO BE THE NORM, LEADING TO UNQUESTIONING ACCEPTANCE OF POTENTIAL INEQUALITIES AND HARM.

LISA DOWNING

Check out the **Further Reading** section for a number of great materials that have been developed by queer theorists and activists that help to reveal heteronormativity.

INSIDE/OUT

In her introduction to the queer theory collection, *Inside/Out* (1991), Diana Fuss analysed the heterosexual/homosexual binary using Derrida's idea of the *supplement*. The supplement is the term that seems to be an *addition* to the "original" term but on which the "original" actually depends. For example, madness, emotionality, and homosexuality are all supplements: you can't have the concept of sanity without madness, rationality without emotionality, or heterosexuality without homosexuality.

Like Butler's performativity, this theory demonstrates how precarious and contingent the supposed norm actually is.

COMING OUT

Fuss particularly focuses on the association between the hetero/homo binary and inside/outside-ness. This relates both to being inside/outside mainstream society, and the focus on gay people "coming out". Fuss suggests that this kind of "outness" is limited because it acknowledges the central place of heterosexuality, and shores up its hierarchical position. People wouldn't have to come out if heterosexuality wasn't the assumed norm.

There are echoes here of Butler's criticism of feminism's reliance on the category of "woman". Coming out as gay risks reinforcing the hierarchical binary structure that underlies heteronormativity and homophobia. It also marginalizes those who remain "in" the closet. There are similar problems with attempts to invert the hierarchy (e.g. saying that gay people are better than straights).

Arguably, then, the focus should be on *revealing* the ways in which this hierarchical binary structure operates, and the other hierarchies of power and knowledge involved in this.

SEDGWICK: HOW TO BRING YOUR KIDS UP GAY

Another key figure in queer theory, Eve Kosofsky Sedgwick, further explores the network of supporting oppositions relating to the heterosexual/homosexual binary.

In her essay "How to Bring Your Kids Up Gay" (1991), Sedgwick highlights the inextricable link between binary sexuality and binary gender. She points out that "acceptable" homosexuality is founded on gender conformity through an analysis of the ways in which "effeminate" gay boys and men continue to be stigmatized and pathologized (in the mainstream media, in medicine, and in gay culture).

THE EPISTEMOLOGY OF THE CLOSET

In her book, *The Epistemology of the Closet* (1990), Sedgwick argues that we need to disentangle sexuality and gender, otherwise heteronormativity remains in place.

NATURE/NURTURE

Sedgwick also explores recent shifts in the nature/nurture binary from regarding sexuality as "social" to "biological", and how the homosexual side of the binary is problematized whichever side of nature/nurture holds sway. She points out that biological "explanations" of sexuality generally explain homosexuality in terms of excess or deficiency, and never endeavour to explain why people are heterosexual.

ASSUMED NORMS

Psychology professor Peter Hegarty's research nicely illuminates what Sedgwick, Fuss, and other queer theorists are saying here: he found that psychological journal articles, and everyday people, tend to assume a male, heterosexual norm and explain women/gay differences as deviations from that norm. Hegarty also found that people are no less homophobic if they believe in nature rather than nurture – supporting Sedgwick's idea that the heterosexual/homosexual hierarchy remains whichever side of the nature/nurture binary is currently stronger.

QUEER BEYOND SEXUALITY AND GENDER

So now you've met some of the founders of queer theory (whether or not they saw themselves that way!) and learnt more about some of its key ideas:

- That identity is neither essential nor fixed but feels this way through repeated performance.
- That normativities are kept in place through associations between binary oppositions.
- That all of this is embedded within current economic and social structures and how power operates within these.

I DON'T MIND MY LEGS AND ARMS AND BODY BEING STUFFED, BECAUSE I CANNOT GET HURT... BUT I DO NOT WANT PEOPLE TO CALL ME A FOOL, AND IF MY HEAD STAYS STUFFED WITH STRAW INSTEAD OF WITH BRAINS, AS YOURS IS, HOW AM I EVER TO KNOW ANYTHING?

THIS SMART/FOOLISH DISTINCTION IS JUST ANOTHER FALSE BINARY...

IDENTITY IS NOT A BUNCH OF LITTLE CUBBYHOLES STUFFED RESPECTIVELY WITH INTELLECT, RACE, SEX, CLASS, VOCATION, GENDER. IDENTITY FLOWS BETWEEN, OVER, ASPECTS OF A PERSON. IDENTITY IS A RIVER - A PROCESS.

GLORIA ANZALDÚA

Of course, all of this applies to many other identities, binaries, and normativities beyond those associated with sexuality and gender. For this reason, queer theory has been straining at the confines of a narrow understanding of queer from the start.

QUEER ENGAGEMENTS

Now let's look at a few of the areas that queer theory has engaged with: how people have put queer theory to work.

Because queer theory generally came out the humanities, many of its academic studies have focused on literature, media, and other *texts*. Over the next few pages we've focused on how queer theory has engaged with popular culture because:

THE TEXTS MIGHT ALREADY BE FAMILIAR TO YOU.

POPULAR CULTURE IS A KEY AREA OF ENGAGEMENT WITH QUEER THEORY.

YOU MAY GET IDEAS ABOUT HOW YOU COULD THINK MORE QUEERLY ABOUT THE CULTURAL TEXTS AROUND YOU.

FOCUS ON TEXTS

Many of the classic early queer theory books involved the writers doing "close readings" of literary, cultural, political, or other texts, and more recent queer theory has continued this trend. This is because queer theory – and post-structuralism more widely – takes language very seriously. It's *through* language that certain "knowledges" about sexuality, gender, and identity are (re)produced.*

EQUAL RIGHTS MANIFESTO

We believe that all — *binary oppositions*

individuals – man (or) woman,

black (or) white, gay (or)[1] straight —

deserve the same* set of — *suggests equivalence between gender, race, sexuality*

(basic human rights.) → *human / non-human split implied*

We may be born different — *biological essentialism?*

but we should be treated

equally.

1 Excludes bisexuality, non-binary, mixed race experience

---

* The brackets here mean that knowledges are both produced and reproduced through language – in fact we could argue that production is always really a reproduction of something that already exists – so we use "(re)produced".

DISCOURSE ANALYSIS

Queer theory frequently involves a kind of critical engagement called *discourse analysis*. This interrogates linguistic, and visual, texts by asking these kinds of questions of them:

PLAYING WITH LANGUAGE

This focus on language is probably one of the reasons why queer theorists enjoy wordplay so much. You can see this from the titles of some of the pages in this book (many of which we've taken from queer theory books). Queer theorists are forever putting brackets in the middle of words,* cracking puns, or getting excited about words which have multiple meanings.

HMM, "DRAG" CAN REFER TO TIME PASSING SLOWLY, OR TO PULLING SOMETHING ALONG WITH YOU, OR IT CAN MEAN PERFORMING A DIFFERENT GENDER.

ELIZABETH FREEMAN

WE "ORIENT" TO SOMETHING WHEN WE TURN TOWARDS IT IN SPACE, BUT WE ALSO USE THE TERM TO REFER TO EXOTIC OTHERNESS (THE ORIENT), AND TO SEXUAL ORIENTATION.

SARA AHMED

TO BE "AGAINST" SOMETHING CAN MEAN BEING IN OPPOSITION TO IT, OR TOUCHING UP ALONGSIDE IT, SO WHAT MIGHT IT MEAN TO BE "AGAINST LOVE"?

LAURA KIPNIS

* Like "(re)produced" a couple of pages back.

QUEERING

Queer reading, or analysis, is often called "*queering*" as it frequently involves rendering a text queerer by reading it in a certain way. Queer theorists and post-structuralists would argue that there's never one "true" reading of any text – not even the one the author intended. Rather, there are always many possible readings, and the reader is implicated in the meanings that are (re)produced. As Foucault said, we are agents of the systems of power and knowledge that are in place, as well as being effects of them.

Also, the potential for reading a text queerly – or otherwise – changes over time as culture changes. For example, current representations of the Holmes–Watson relationship have to explicitly address its queer potential in a way that hasn't always been necessary, due to cultural shifts.

QUEER MOMENTS

Queer theorist Alexander Doty challenged the kinds of analyses done in lesbian and gay studies – which often focused explicitly on LG media, or the reception of mainstream media by LG audiences (therefore presuming identity categories). He argued that *anybody* could experience queer moments when engaging with texts, and that they could happen in otherwise heteronormative texts.

Queer moments are those that disrupt the narrative and destabilize heteronormativity by highlighting what is integral to it: moments which demonstrate that gender is performative, that identities are not fixed, or that queer attractions are possible; or which trouble binary understandings of sexuality and gender.

WHEN JAMES BOND EMERGES FROM THE OCEAN IN **CASINO ROYALE** (2006), IT REFERENCES THE SCENE FROM **DR. NO** (1962) WHERE HONEY RYDER DOES THE SAME. THIS IS A QUEER MOMENT IN ITS INVITATION TO VIEW A MALE BODY WITH A DESIRING GAZE USUALLY DIRECTED AT FEMALE BODIES IN MAINSTREAM MEDIA. THROUGH ITS HYPER-MASCULINITY, IT ALSO DEMONSTRATES THAT MASCULINITY IS AS PERFORMATIVE AS FEMININITY.

CAMP

Camp often involves explicit parody, exaggeration, theatricality, irony, and humour. In this way, camp representations have the potential to demonstrate the performativity of gender and sexuality, and to disrupt normative representations.

However, some have argued that camp has become such a mainstream element of popular culture that it has lost its critical edge and been severed from its history in gay male subculture.

HALBERSTAM AND LOW THEORY

One queer theorist who has produced a lot of work queering popular culture is Jack Halberstam. Halberstam's work values "low" theory and culture as highly as it does "high" theory and culture.* He takes examples from popular culture – such as Disney films, "dumb" comedies, and Lady Gaga – and brings these into conversation with more academic theories. He takes them just as seriously as other scholars do "high" art or literature. At the same time, he treats everything playfully.

In *The Queer Art of Failure* (2011) Halberstam looks to low culture for alternatives to heteronormative understandings of what counts as "success" (marriage, kids, money, house, etc.). Low culture allows representations where things are not taken too seriously, where people mess up, and where forms of resistance can develop which might not otherwise have been thought of.

FOUCAULT VS GAGA

JACK HALBERSTAM

* And yes, he does trouble this low/high binary too.

"DUDE, WHERE'S MY GENDER?"

Halberstam compares the film *Dude, Where's My Car?* (2000) to other "bromance" movies about pairs of stupid white men. Many such films are resolved by one or both of the men having to "grow up" and engage in heteronormativity, usually by "getting the girl" and distancing from the friendship.

In this film, however, the trope of having their memories erased allows the main characters to remain in a state of forgetfulness, and – through their "stupidity" – heteronormativity is challenged. The characters blur the boundaries between homosociality (male buddies) and homosexuality (being naked together and kissing each other), and also form friendships with gay and trans characters.

COLLECTIVISM IN *FINDING NEMO*

Halberstam also considers how the Pixar movie, *Finding Nemo* (2003), differs from earlier Disney films. These often involved heteronormative love stories, or a hero using their power to restore balance to a (hetero)normative family. The Pixar movies generally involve more collectivist ideals and value friendship over (hetero)romantic relationships. Consider the characters in *Toy Story* (1995) or *Monsters, Inc.* (2001).

Halberstam examines how the forgetful character of Dory – appropriately voiced by Ellen Degeneres – offers a way of resisting (hetero)normative ideals of family. Dory can't remain part of a conventional "biological" family because she's forgotten them, and she can't form a romantic relationship with the male character because she'd instantly forget him. However, she happily bonds with all kinds of creatures in a way that isn't constrained by biology, romantic love, or linear time.

QUEER ART

As well as critically engaging with existing texts, queer theory can also creatively engage with popular culture by producing new texts. Artistic forms can, in themselves, be recognized as valid ways of knowing, thinking through, and experiencing queer worlds.

For example, the science fiction novels of Octavia Butler and the comics of Alison Bechdel explicitly incorporate queer theory ideas into fictional writing. In New Queer Cinema, directors such as Gus Van Sant and Rose Troche theorize about queerness through their films. Queercore and queer hip hop genres offer similar possibilities in the arena of music.

GUERRILLA TACTICS

Queer art engagements are not all on the level of publicly recognized media. Some great queer interventions happen online in the form of, for example, collective snarky responses to heteronormative products, parodies of heteronormative music videos, and fan fic *shipping* and *slashing* of heteronormative characters.

Shipping and slashing involve writing otherwise non-involved characters into relation(ship)s – depicted by a slash or portmanteau name, such as Buffy/Willow or Drarry (Draco and Harry). Slashing and shipping turn queer readings of texts into queer writings. Part of the pleasure is in interspersing queerer stories between the gaps in the canon of mainstream media texts. A well-known example of such slashy queer writing is *Wicked* (1995/2003), which imagines a whole different story going on between the scenes of *The [Wonderful] Wizard of Oz* (1900/1939), destabilizing the narratives and binaries involved in the original.

SUCH INTERVENTIONS BRING PLEASURE AND PLAYFULNESS INTO COMBINATION WITH CRITICAL QUEER ENGAGEMENT.

QUEER BIOLOGY

A very different queer engagement to that with popular culture has been the burgeoning of what we might call queer biology.

Remember Alfred Kinsey whose approach was pretty compatible with queer theory? Since his work in the mid-20th century, most of the science of gender and sexuality has taken a far more biologically essentialist, and binary, approach, and has therefore been critiqued, rather than engaged with, by queer theory.

NATURE/NURTURE

As a *social constructionist* approach, queer theory is often taken to be on the "nurture" side of the nature/nurture debate (yet another problematic binary), engaging as it does in a process of *denaturalizing* social categories.

Foucault and Butler never said that there was *no* role for biology in our sexuality or gender. They were simply more interested in how sexuality and gender were historically and culturally produced as constructed categories of experience. Also, they were rightly sceptical of biology when it made claims which were:

- *Essentialist*: our identities are fixed

- *Reductionist*: all gender/sexuality experience can be reduced to our biology (hormones, brain activity)

- *Determinist*: people's gender/ sexuality is determined by their genetics, hormones, and/or physiology.*

ON THE QUESTION OF BIOLOGY, I HAVE ABSOLUTELY NOTHING TO SAY.

* Social theories can also be essentialist, reductionist, and determinist if they see our identities as rooted in, determined by, and fixed because of social aspects of experience (such as upbringing).

THE HETERONORMATIVE GAZE OF SCIENCE

In recent years, however, biologists such as Anne Fausto-Sterling, Joan Roughgarden, and Sari van Anders have worked on sex and gender in ways that are far more compatible with queer theory: emphasizing diversity and fluidity, and eschewing essentialism, reductionism, and determinism.

One focus of queer biology has been on challenging taken-for-granted scientific (and popular) notions that heteronormativity is "natural" (biologically based and evolved due to the need for procreation), and that therefore all non-human animals are heterosexual and conform to stereotypical gender roles.

EVOLUTION'S RAINBOW AND *BIOLOGICAL EXUBERANCE*

Bruce Baghemil's book *Biological Exuberance* (1999) documents same-sex sexual behaviour across 450 species. In *Evolution's Rainbow* (2004) Joan Roughgarden argues that the social function of sex is at least as important as its reproductive function among animals, strengthening bonds between individuals, and within a group. Pleasure is clearly important for both human and non-human animals. Many animals masturbate, have sex when already pregnant, and engage in other non-procreative sexual activities.

Also, over 4,000 species reproduce asexually, without a partner, and many species change sex during their lifetime. This is so common in fish that fish which do not change sex are regarded as rather unusual.

SEXING THE BODY

In *Sexing the Body* (2000), geneticist Anne Fausto-Sterling found diverse variations in sex/gender in humans.

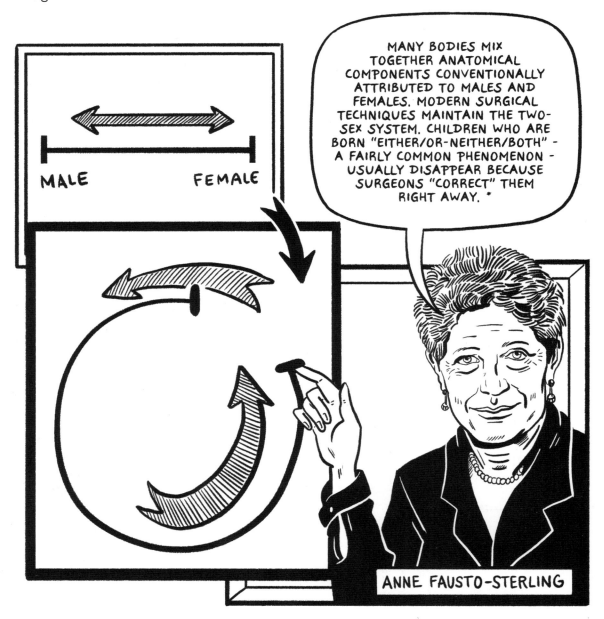

MANY BODIES MIX TOGETHER ANATOMICAL COMPONENTS CONVENTIONALLY ATTRIBUTED TO MALES AND FEMALES. MODERN SURGICAL TECHNIQUES MAINTAIN THE TWO-SEX SYSTEM. CHILDREN WHO ARE BORN "EITHER/OR-NEITHER/BOTH" - A FAIRLY COMMON PHENOMENON - USUALLY DISAPPEAR BECAUSE SURGEONS "CORRECT" THEM RIGHT AWAY. *

MALE   FEMALE

ANNE FAUSTO-STERLING

When it comes to gender, there's actually diversity across all levels of biology: in chromosomal make-up, in hormonal sensitivity and take-up, in genitals (such that it's not always clear what is a penis or a clitoris), in brain chemistry and structure, and in all physical aspects that people think of as "male" or "female". Many people fit more on the "opposite" end of the spectrum than would be predicted by gender stereotypes (e.g. hairiness, height, voice pitch, strength, and chest size).

* This practice is now challenged by activists and medics.

DELUSIONS OF GENDER

Another of Fausto-Sterling's books is titled *Sex/Gender* (2012) because, like Butler, she challenges the nature/nurture split between (biological) sex and (social) gender (roles).

Neuroscientist Cordelia Fine also challenges this split. Her *Delusions of Gender* (2010) makes a compelling case that, rather than being "hardwired", gender roles become written on our brains through the kind of repetition of gender normative social practices that Butler wrote about.

Fine draws on extensive evidence from both neuroscientific and psychological studies, demonstrating how much more gender stereotyped people's performance, attitudes, and behaviour become when they're primed to be aware of gender, and how such habits shape neural connections over time (neuroplasticity).

BIOPSYCHOSOCIAL

So, there are now biological approaches which are consistent with queer theory, and the idea that sexuality and gender are socially constructed. These *biopsychosocial* approaches consider our biological, psychological, and social worlds as overlapping, intrinsically linked, and impossible to tease apart (hence the compound word: biopsychosocial). All elements impact on each other in a complex web or network.

Queer biologists are interested in how these elements operate together to produce sexual and gender diversity and fluidity. A very oversimplified* example might look something like this.

*Because actually we could never separate the individual elements or determine cause-and-effect relationships in this way.

SEXUAL CONFIGURATIONS

Sari van Anders's sexual configurations theory is a major biopsychosocial theory of sexuality with its roots firmly in queer biology. Van Anders explicitly rejects biological essentialism, reductionism, and determinism, pointing out that our neuroendocrinology (testosterone levels, for example) can both influence behaviour and/or be altered by it.

She brings together queer and feminist theory with bioscientific research to put forward a testable, empirically-grounded framework of sexuality that is multi-dimensional (not just about gender of attraction), dynamic and fluid (not fixed and immutable), socially situated, and resonant with people's actual lived experience.

So, each of us has a unique *sexual configuration* (rather than a shared *sexual orientation*). We may also configure differently or similarly for different aspects of relationships (e.g. erotic/nurturant aspects).

CRITICAL SEXOLOGY

A further form of queer engagement could broadly be termed "critical sexology". Remember that sexology refers to two things, which are interlinked, given that some sexologists are involved with both:

- The academic study of human sex and sexuality (often in the social sciences such as psychology and sociology, as well as in the sciences).
- Applied professional practice in this area, such as sexual medicine, sexual health, and sex therapy.

Critical sexology explicitly aims to bring queer theory into conversation with these two areas: the study and practice of sexology.

FEATURES OF CRITICAL SEXOLOGY

Critical forms of sexology generally share the following common features:

- Bringing together work from across multiple disciplines
- Non-pathologizing and non-essentializing stances
- Emphasizing diversity
- Seeing all forms of sexuality and sexual representations – normative and non-normative – as equally subject to (academic) scrutiny
- Locating all identities and practices within wider social structures and power dynamics
- An ethics of accountability to those being represented in research and theory.

Many critical sexologists also try to shape policy and practice in these areas through direct engagement with sexual/gender communities.

THINKING FROM THE MARGINS

Like Sari van Anders, several of these scholars endeavour to think *from* the sexual margins: valuing the insights that can be gained from groups and individuals who are critically engaging with their standpoints, and often thinking creatively about sex, gender, and relationships.

This is in stark contrast to much past sexology research and theory, which endeavoured to universalize and *explain* those regarded as "different" or "abnormal".

Critical sexologists are more likely than queer theorists in the humanities to study *lived experiences*. Therefore, they often take a *psychosocial* approach, bringing queer theory together with phenomenological, psychodynamic, or other more experiential forms of research.

KINK

Critical research on kink or BDSM (Bondage and Discipline, Dominance and Submission, and SadoMasochism) has challenged the previous sexology focus on delineating normal from abnormal (paraphilic) forms of sex.

From a queer perspective, this research is also important for shifting focus from sexual *identities* to sexual *practices*; gender of attraction to other dimensions of sexuality; PIV sex to other sexual and non-sexual activities.

Such research has demonstrated that those involved in BDSM are no more "psychologically unhealthy" than anybody else, and has provided rich accounts of the lived experience of kinksters within the current cultural context (which continues to pathologize, criminalize, and stigmatize them).

SPANKING, FOR EXAMPLE, CAN MEAN: TAKING ON A DIFFERENT ROLE FOR A WHILE, BEING PLAYFUL AND SILLY, RELAXATION, AN ENDORPHIN RUSH, DEMONSTRATING HOW MUCH YOU'RE CAPABLE OF ENDURING, EXPLORING SOMETHING TRAUMATIC FROM THE PAST, BUILDING INTIMACY WITH ANOTHER PERSON, LETTING YOURSELF BE NURTURED...

OPEN NON-MONOGAMY

Critical research on openly non-monogamous relationships has focused on potentially queer ways of relating, pointing out that heteronormativity inherently includes *mononormativity*: privileging of monogamous, couple-based relationship forms.

Just as Halberstam explores queer relating potentials in popular media, sexologists study people in open, polyamorous, or otherwise non-monogamous relationships.

As with same-sex attraction, from a queer perspective it's important to point out that neither kink practices nor openly non-monogamous relationships are transgressive per se. Some scholars have been criticized for replacing the sex negative, pathologizing stance of previous sexology with a wholly sex positive, celebratory stance, which is just as problematic and depends on a binary.

QUEERING SEXUAL MEDICINE

Some critical sexologists have engaged directly with medicine and psychotherapy, questioning diagnoses and clinical practices employed in the past with trans and intersex* people, often on the basis of heteronormative assumptions about sex/gender.

Critical psychologists Lih Mei Liao and Katrina Roen have collaborated with queer scholar Iain Morland to document the histories and current experiences of treatment of intersex people. They also practice alongside medics, influencing policy.

Key issues they have highlighted include how to ensure consent in surgical procedures, the implications of evidence that many people don't experience and express their gender in binary ways, and how vital it is to validate this for psychological well-being.

* Also called diverse sex development (DSD).

QUEERING SEX THERAPY

Critical sex therapists, such as the contributors to Peggy Kleinplatz's *New Directions in Sex Therapy* (2012), have pointed out the heteronormativity of existing categories of sexual "dysfunction" and the inherent assumption that sex = PIV sex. Instead of categorizing sexual "dysfunctions", they suggest that any sexual experience (including erections, orgasms, or their lack) has different meanings for different people, related to the relationships and wider culture that they're embedded in. Therefore, instead of "treatment" of problems, the therapeutic task becomes understanding clients' experiences and what they mean for them within their context.

They also see sexual difficulties occurring within wider "master narratives" about sex. People often struggle to be present in the sexual moment because of a "hidden curriculum" of social rules they feel they should follow around what constitutes "good" or "proper" sex.

CRITICISMS AND TENSIONS

Now let's turn our attention to some of the major issues with queer theory. Many of the criticisms and tensions only apply to certain thinkers, or strands of thought, rather than to the whole of queer theory (because that would be impossible). Some of them also apply more to queer activisms than they do to queer theories. However, they're all important issues to attend to and grapple with.

A particularly vital set of criticisms and tensions has emerged as a result of considering queer theory together with race. Teresa de Lauretis, who coined the term "queer theory", put race right at the heart of the endeavour because sexual subjectivity is shaped by race just as much as gender.

However, few of the queer theories we have covered so far have considered race as centrally important (and, relatedly, how many of the queer theorists mentioned have been white?). Queer theory has therefore been criticized for "white-washing", and an ongoing rigorous analysis of how queer theory and activism is structured by whiteness is required.

WHY SHOULD RACE BE CENTRAL TO QUEER THEORY?

- Many of the first people to highlight the problems with an identity politics based around a singular identity were black feminists.
- As Gloria Anzaldúa pointed out, race categories are one vital way in which people are identified and policed (in fixed, binary, biologically essentialist ways), at least as much as gender or sexuality.
- Race emerged as a "scientific" classificatory concept around the same time as sexuality, and – as Foucault pointed out – attempts to define and ensure "racial purity" were inextricably linked to the construction of gender and sexuality. For example, regarding homosexuality as wasting the possibility of white reproduction, and women who had sex outside of (white) marriage as impure or deviant.

INTERROGATING RACE

Gender, race, and sexuality therefore come together in terms of the "norm" of humanness against which others are compared: generally a white, heterosexual, cisgender man. For example, black and Asian people are often regarded as at polar extremes from white people in relation to gender/sexuality. Asian men are stereotyped as feminine and black men as hypermasculine; Asian women are stereotyped as innocent and black women as hypersexual.

RACE SHOULD BE JUST AS SUBJECT TO QUEER THEORETICAL INTERROGATION AS GENDER AND SEXUALITY.

CATHY COHEN

RESPONSES TO THIS MARGINALIZATION OF RACE

Critical race theory acknowledges how racism is engrained in societal systems and structures, rather than locating it in individuals. It analyses how white privilege and supremacy perpetuate the marginalization of people of colour.

Postcolonial theory aims to analyse and disrupt colonial binaries such as colonizer/colonized, dominant/subordinate, oppressor/oppressed, and highlights the violence that they're implicated in.

I DEVELOPED QUARE STUDIES SPECIFICALLY TO EXAMINE THE EXPERIENCES OF QUEER PEOPLE OF COLOUR.

QUARE STUDIES
E. PATRICK JOHNSON

BRINGING TOGETHER CRITICAL RACE THEORY AND QUEER THEORY ENABLES US TO EXPLORE WHAT IT MEANS TO DISIDENTIFY WITH DIFFERENT ASPECTS OF IDENTITIES - ESPECIALLY FOR THOSE WITH IDENTITIES THAT ARE TYPICALLY MARGINALIZED.

CRITICAL RACE THEORY
JOSÉ ESTEBAN MUÑOZ

POST-COLONIAL THEORY
SCOTT MORGENSEN

I BRING TOGETHER POSTCOLONIAL THEORY AND QUEER THEORY TO EXAMINE HOW WHITE COLONIZATION OF INDIGENOUS PEOPLE IN NORTH AMERICA OFTEN INVOLVED THE MURDER OF TWO-SPIRIT PEOPLE, WHO WERE VIEWED AS SEXUAL AND GENDER DEVIANTS.

Of course, race is not the only additional cultural category that operates with gender and sexuality in these kinds of interlocking ways. Other examples include: class, ethnicity, nationality, age, disability, and religious affiliation ... an exhaustive list is impossible.

This presents a challenge for all theoretical approaches that focus primarily on one of these categories – this often leads to neglect of the others.

* With gratitude to Flavia Dzodan, whose original quote related to feminism.

WHITE MINORITY-WORLD FOCUS

Related to these criticisms around race are criticisms of queer theory for drawing predominantly on theories developed in a white minority-world context. The term "minority world" reminds us that a majority of people live in the economically poorer continents (Asia, Africa, and Latin America), reflecting another set of (global) inequalities. As always, the binary distinction is overly simplistic, as there is diversity within the majority world, and some countries blur the minority/majority boundary.

One issue with a white minority-world focus is that – as anthropologist Gilbert Herdt points out – many cultures globally don't view gender and sexuality in the essentialist, binary ways common in the minority world.

HIJRA ↑

TOM / DEE ↑

← BISSU

A MAJORITY OF QUEER THEORIES REFLECT THE VIEWS AND CONCERNS OF A MINORITY OF THE WORLD'S CULTURES. THEY EXCLUDE THE HIJRA IDENTITY IN INDIA; THE TOM, DEE, AND KATHOEY IDENTITIES IN THAILAND; THE BISSU, CALABAI, AND CALALAI IDENTITIES IN INDONESIA...

GILBERT HERDT →

SOUTHERN THEORY

Gender theorist Raewyn Connell has turned her attention in recent years to "Southern theory": the knowledges and ideas that have emerged from indigenous Australia, Africa, Latin America, and Asia. For example, it seems odd that queer theory has rarely included a sustained engagement with Buddhist philosophy.*

Of course many versions of Buddhism have still managed to think in binary ways about gender and to be rather sex-negative.

* Later works by both Foucault and Sedgwick do begin to engage with this.

QUEER GOES GLOBAL

Other thinkers have focused on:

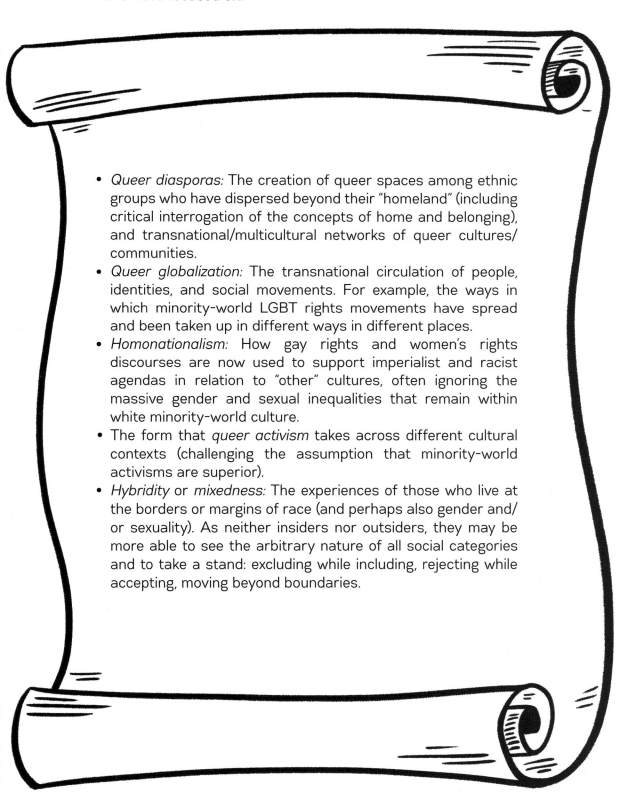

- *Queer diasporas:* The creation of queer spaces among ethnic groups who have dispersed beyond their "homeland" (including critical interrogation of the concepts of home and belonging), and transnational/multicultural networks of queer cultures/communities.
- *Queer globalization:* The transnational circulation of people, identities, and social movements. For example, the ways in which minority-world LGBT rights movements have spread and been taken up in different ways in different places.
- *Homonationalism:* How gay rights and women's rights discourses are now used to support imperialist and racist agendas in relation to "other" cultures, often ignoring the massive gender and sexual inequalities that remain within white minority-world culture.
- The form that *queer activism* takes across different cultural contexts (challenging the assumption that minority-world activisms are superior).
- *Hybridity* or *mixedness:* The experiences of those who live at the borders or margins of race (and perhaps also gender and/or sexuality). As neither insiders nor outsiders, they may be more able to see the arbitrary nature of all social categories and to take a stand: excluding while including, rejecting while accepting, moving beyond boundaries.

STRATEGIC ESSENTIALISM

From these kinds of engagements we can return to queer theory's anti-essentialist and anti-identity politics stance in a somewhat more critical way.

Critical theorist Gayatri Chakravorty Spivak developed the concept of "strategic essentialism" to capture the idea that it's sometimes advantageous for marginalized groups to temporarily "essentialize" themselves: foregrounding their group identity in simplified ways in order to achieve their goals, or to prevent assimilation.

STRATEGIC ESSENTIALISM MIGHT INVOLVE, FOR EXAMPLE, REMAINING QUIET ABOUT THE DIFFERENCES BETWEEN INDIVIDUALS WITHIN THE GROUP AS THEY FIGHT FOR A COMMON GOAL, DESPITE ENGAGING IN THOSE DEBATES PRIVATELY.

GAYATRI CHAKRAVORTY SPIVAK

A PLACE FOR IDENTITY POLITICS AFTER ALL?

Strategic essentialism allows us to reconsider the value of fixed identities.

Alan Sinfield highlights the gains that have been made by campaigns for LGBT rights based on an "identity politics" model. It enables marginalized groups to claim spaces for self-expression and to lobby the state for rights and concessions. So, perhaps identity politics can be politically effective. Elizabeth Grosz and others have argued that we need to engage with *both* identity *and* queer politics if we're to realize political success.*

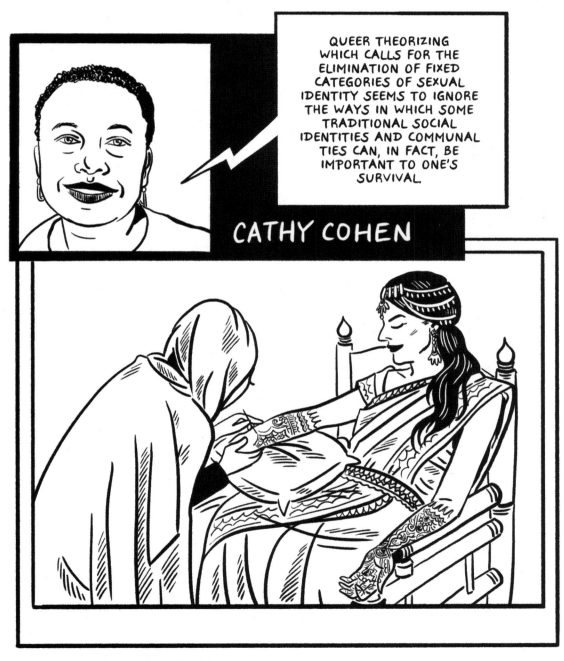

QUEER THEORIZING WHICH CALLS FOR THE ELIMINATION OF FIXED CATEGORIES OF SEXUAL IDENTITY SEEMS TO IGNORE THE WAYS IN WHICH SOME TRADITIONAL SOCIAL IDENTITIES AND COMMUNAL TIES CAN, IN FACT, BE IMPORTANT TO ONE'S SURVIVAL.

CATHY COHEN

* A manoeuvre away from yet another binary.

QUEER AND BISEXUALITY

One place in which the queer theory–identity politics tension has particularly played out is in relation to bisexuality. Bisexual scholarship and activism has highlighted the *erasure* or *invisibility* of bisexuality within mainstream culture, due to binary understandings of sexuality: seeing people as either gay or straight. The implications of this include:

- *Biphobia:* discrimination against bisexual people for being supposedly untrustworthy, greedy, or confused.
- *Double discrimination:* from both heterosexual and LG people, meaning that bi people often feel that they don't fit anywhere, and have to keep (re)coming out as bi.
- Higher rates of mental health problems among bisexual people than heterosexual, L or G people.

ERASING BISEXUALITY

You might think that queer theory would embrace those whose experience of attraction to more than one gender* disrupts binary understandings of sexuality (and often gender). Also, most bisexual scholarship and activism has an explicitly queer – rather than identity politics – approach, and has much to offer to queer theorists, particularly around how to navigate (in)visibility queerly.

However, queer theory very rarely engages with bisexuality, and often furthers its erasure. Psychoanalysis relegates it to the past (a stage on the way to mature binary sexuality). Queer theory relegates it to some utopian future when there will be no need to label sexualities, and refuses to acknowledge current bisexual experience.

* The most common definition of bisexuality within bi communities; many take the "bi" to mean attraction to people of both the "same gender" and "other genders".

QUEER AND FEMINISM

Historically, there have been tensions between queer theory and some forms of feminism because each has engaged with gender and sexuality differently. Some tensions date back to the "feminist sex wars", with queer theorists critiquing feminisms that regard sexuality purely through the lens of patriarchal gender relations.

Certainly there are obvious incompatibilities between queer theory and any feminism that relies on binary categories of men and women, and/or the idea that these are essential characteristics of a person.

At their most vitriolic, feminists such as Camille Paglia labelled queer theorists "flimflamming freeloaders", and Martha Nussbaum described Judith Butler as a "collaborator with evil" for not attending to the material realities of the lives of battered women or LG people lacking legal protections.

QUEER THEORIST VS. FEMINIST

PENIS FITS VAGINA; NO FANCY LINGUISTIC GAME-PLAYING CAN CHANGE THAT BIOLOGIC FACT!

CAMILLE PAGLIA

ARE YOU SURE ABOUT THAT?

ANNE FAUSTO-STERLING

QUEER FEMINISM?

Judith Butler's (queer) theories certainly posed a challenge for much feminism in arguing that anything which perpetuates the notion of "women" as a stable, unified identity risks solidifying the gendered structures of oppression rather than liberating people from it.

However, sociology professor Diane Richardson suggests that too much is made of the contrasts and antagonisms between queer theory and feminism. It's a false binary divide given how many activists and scholars are both feminist and queer. She suggests that there's much to be gained from bringing queer tools of deconstruction into dialogue with feminist concerns for justice.

QUEER MASCULINITY

There's also some concern from feminists that queer theorists risk paying insufficient attention to gender in their analyses of sexuality. Annamarie Jagose, for example, raises the potential that:

If queer theorists don't attend enough to the masculine-centric culture in which they live, they could end up reproducing it, for example by overly focusing on gay men and masculinities.

Julia Serano writes about how this plays out in some queer activist circles where there can be far greater acceptance and celebration of trans masculinity than of trans femininity, and also femmephobia (where femininity is treated as *more* performative – and therefore somehow more suspect – than masculinity, due to wider cultural narratives).

QUEER AND TRANS: THE TERF WARS

The question of queer theory and trans has been one key aspect of the contestations between feminism and queer theory, again circling around the question of whether gender is essential or constructed.*

Surprisingly – given their often essentialist views of womanhood – some *trans-exclusionary radical feminists (TERFs)* have used Judith Butler's work to further their agendas. Janice Raymond and Sheila Jeffreys have argued that trans surgeries are a form of mutilation, carried out for political reasons because of the way gender is constructed in male-dominated society. Trans people are often represented here as dupes of heteronormative medical discourses who could – and should – *choose* to remain in their assigned gender to challenge rigid gender roles, rather than transitioning.

* Another problematic binary, as you've seen.

BUTLER ON TRANS

Butler strongly refutes TERF arguments as based on a misunderstanding of social constructionism. As we've seen, gender being socially constructed does not mean that a person's felt sense of their gender is somehow not *real* or that they could easily *choose* it to be otherwise. Nor does it mean that there's no bodily element to human experience. Butler argues against any kind of feminist policing of trans lives.

IT IS ALWAYS BRAVE TO INSIST ON UNDERGOING TRANSFORMATIONS THAT FEEL NECESSARY. ALL OF US, AS BODIES, ARE IN THE ACTIVE POSITION OF FIGURING OUT HOW TO LIVE WITH AND AGAINST THE NORMS THAT HELP TO FORM US. ONE SHOULD BE FREE TO DETERMINE THE COURSE OF ONE'S GENDERED LIFE.

CO-OPTING TRANS EXPERIENCE?

Author of *Second Skins: The Body Narratives of Transsexuality* (1998) Jay Prosser asserts that trans experience has been central to the development of queer theory. This is intriguing given queer theory's lack of engagement with bi experience and the fact that many trans people do experience themselves very much within binary gender categories and as essentially men/women – although, of course, others do not.

Gender clinician and scholar Christina Richards argues that queer theory risks falling into another set of binaries with trans experience: depicting it in *either* highly celebratory or highly critical ways, as *either* subversive or conforming.

TRANS STUDIES

Co-opting trans people's experiences to support any particular theory does a disservice to them, as well as presenting a diverse group as somehow unified, and, again, sidestepping the very real material challenges and discriminations facing trans people.

Often drawing on queer theory, the burgeoning area of trans studies produces rich accounts of the lived experiences of trans people, which resist simple, unifying narratives. Trans studies academic Jacob Hale's suggestions for writing about trans are a useful starting point for such work.

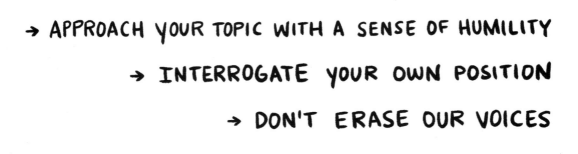

→ APPROACH YOUR TOPIC WITH A SENSE OF HUMILITY

→ INTERROGATE YOUR OWN POSITION

→ DON'T ERASE OUR VOICES

→ DON'T ASSUME THAT ALL TRANS EXPERIENCES ARE THE SAME

GENDERQUEER

One area of trans that has gained wider attention only relatively recently is genderqueer, or non-binary gender. Both of these words have been used as umbrella terms for an explosion of descriptions of genders that fall between or beyond the gender binary (gender neutral, genderfluid, agender, pangender, and androgynous, to name just a few). This kind of gender explosion was exactly what Sandra Bem proposed was needed to dismantle gender inequality.

It seems likely that there will be similar tensions between queer theory and non-binary people as there are with bi and trans people. They disrupt the gender binary, but some may be seen as returning to identity politics in rights-based campaigns.

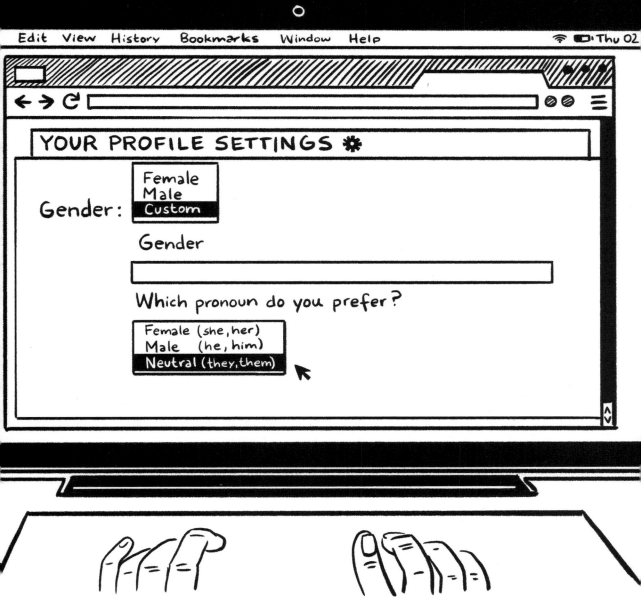

CISGENDERISM

Gender researcher-practitioner Gávi Ansara's concept of cisgenderism is a useful element of heteronormativity to be mindful of when thinking about trans. Cisgenderism is the system of thinking and practice – based on the assumption of a cisgender norm – that invalidates people's own understanding of their genders and bodies, including misgendering, pathologizing, marginalizing, and binarizing people.

Cisgenderism might include: assuming that because a person looks masculine, they were assigned male at birth, or they have certain anatomy; calling this person "sir" or "madam" on the assumption that everyone is either male or female; or asking personal questions about this person's sex life and medical interventions when you find out they're trans.

MATERIALITY MATTERS

You've seen throughout the criticisms of queer theory considered here that many of them centre around underestimating or obscuring the *material* conditions of people's lives, such as poverty, discrimination, violence, and (un)employment. This argument has been made by critical race theorists, feminists, and trans scholars/activists.

Susan A. Mann also argues that class has been an "invisible ghost" in queer theory, due to the absence of analysis of the economic and political contexts in which identity construction and/or destruction take place.

Queer theory has been accused of being too focused on individual acts of transgression and cultural representations. This could be seen as ignoring, or glossing over, the realities of oppressive processes and systematic inequalities that underpin discourse.

LIVED EXPERIENCES

We've also seen that queer theory's arguments against identity politics have been criticized for failing to consider the lived realities of those whose identities have never been fully recognized (e.g. colonized people, bisexual people, trans people).

For these reasons, perhaps queer theory needs to move away from dismissing any form of identity category, to considering both what these categories enable for people *and* what they close down.*

ROSI BRAIDOTTI

ONE CANNOT DECONSTRUCT A SUBJECTIVITY ONE HAS NEVER BEEN FULLY GRANTED. IN ORDER TO ANNOUNCE THE DEATH OF THE SUBJECT ONE MUST FIRST HAVE GAINED THE RIGHT TO SPEAK AS ONE.

I'M JUST LOOKING FOR SOME KIND OF COMMUNITY...

I THINK I MIGHT BE...

PLEASE LISTEN TO OUR VOICES...

*Both/and" thinking is one way of resisting either/or binaries.

INACCESSIBLE?

Perhaps the most well-known criticism of queer theory is that it's inaccessible. Indeed Butler once won an international award for the most incomprehensible academic work! There's a serious point here that if a theory is too abstract, complex, and opaque it will exclude those outside academia from engaging with it. It may also be regarded as elitist and class-biased.

Queer theorists have argued back that academics should be allowed to express sophisticated ideas using complex terminology. Science, for example, is rarely criticized for this.

INEFFECTIVE?

However, it would be tragedy if some of the useful and relevant ideas from queer theory did not filter through people's everyday lives and understandings. Particularly queer theory has a lot to offer to LGBT and feminist activists about how they could organize more effectively and inclusively, for example around gender and sexual diversity rather than identity categories.

Perhaps it's necessary in any area to have both intellectual thinkers and those who can translate their ideas into accessible language, and into everyday lives and politics. Queer activist authors such as Julia Serano, Riki Anne Wilchins, Kate Bornstein, S. Bear Bergman, and Mattilda Bernstein Sycamore have certainly been effective at this so far, and we hope this book might play a small part in that process too.

DRIVEN BY FASHION?

Finally, some criticize queer theory – like much critical theory – as overly driven by fashion. Analysing why queer theory distanced itself from feminism, Janice McLaughlin draws on common cycles of academic debate that she regards as unproductive.

A BODY OF WORK IS *identified as* DOMINATING, EXCLUSIONARY, *and* OUT-OF-DATE.

A new body of WORK DEVELOPS OUT OF THE *identification* OF THESE FAILINGS.

There's often an *increasingly* STEREOTYPICAL presentation of the old WORK, which FAILS to capture its COMPLEXITY, MULTIPLICITY, OR CONTEXT.

ACADEMIC processes are SET UP *around the* NEW BODY OF WORK.

CRITICISMS *start to occur of this* NEW BODY *of* WORK...

Similar processes are at play in activism too. Perhaps the old/new and wrong/right binaries need to be resisted. Otherwise we risk repeating the mistakes of the past; falling into intergenerational "wars"; and remaining insecure about whether we're up-to-date with terminologies, ideas, and practices.

GOOD QUEERS AND BAD NOT-QUEERS

It seems that many of the criticisms of queer theory we have covered here involve it inadvertently falling into other binaries: inside/outside, transgressive/normative, radical/conforming, liberatory/assimilationist. Perhaps nothing illustrates the powerful hold that binary concepts have on our thinking and practices more than the tendency of even ideas that explicitly critique binaries to find themselves conceptualizing things in binary ways.

One new binary that is very hard to resist – in queer theory and activism – is the queer/not queer binary, which maps onto binaries of right/wrong and good/bad. As we've seen, for example, it's easy to fall into cycles of painting past ideas and practices as not-queer-enough and new ideas and practices as queerer and better. Such "queerer than thou" judgements are rarely helpful!

Perhaps it's more useful to see each theory or activism as offering up new possibilities *and* problems, new opportunities *and* restrictions.

W(H)ITHER QUEER THEORY?

Now you've learnt about some of the key criticisms of, and tensions within, queer theory, we'll spend the remainder of the book on some of the directions that queer theory has taken in recent years (sometimes in response to these criticisms/tensions).

Queer theorist Donald E. Hall's play on words "w(h)ither" is useful here as we're asking both where queer theory has gone, as well as whether it has withered. This is an important question, given that people have been asking whether queer theory is obsolete ever since it started!

Here we'll touch upon:

- New normativities (after heteronormativity)
- Recent turns in queer theory (especially the antisocial turn)
- Queer thinking on communities.

THE TROUBLE WITH NORMAL

Rather quickly in the history of queer theory, writers like Michael Warner were discussing the dangers of LGBT moves towards normalcy, conformity, and assimilation such as "same-sex" marriage.

Susan Stryker coined the term "homonormativity" to capture the way in which gay and lesbian became the primary identities associated with LGBT movements in the 80s and 90s (B and T being afterthoughts). Later Lisa Duggan wrote of "a new homonormativity".

We can see homonormativity, for example, in "safe" depictions of (white, male) "gay best friends" and gay parents in TV and films.

THE CRAB BUCKET

The fantasy author Terry Pratchett used the metaphor of the crab bucket to explain normativity. You don't need a lid on a bucket of crabs: if any of the crabs make it over the rim of the bucket, the other crabs will pull it back in. Also the safety and certainty of being in the bucket make it tempting for each crab to remain there.

If we do manage to escape the heteronormative crab bucket, we're in a precarious place – scuttling around on the beach on our own – so it's highly tempting to join another crab bucket, with its own sets of rules and ideologies. Hence homonormativity, and, indeed, binormativity, polynormavity, kinknormativity …

There's a certain irony in people looking over at the mainstream bucket, laughing at the crabs being pulled back in, not realizing that they're doing exactly the same thing.

NEW NORMATIVITIES

David Halperin discusses new normativities within gay male culture: disciplinary regimes, such as clothing, diet, and exercise, whereby people police themselves and each other. Many men are alienated by these, often without recourse to feminist critiques that are somewhat available to women struggling with body policing.

Many people have written critically on same-sex marriage and its colonial, racist, classist, and sexist roots. Dean Spade suggests that there are much queerer ways to fight for the benefits same-sex marriage would confer. These would also be more inclusive of the least privileged people who these things affect most, and who have least access to marriage.

SAME-SEX MARRIAGE ALLOWS PEOPLE TO BENEFIT FROM THEIR PARTNER'S HEALTH BENEFITS, TO GAIN LEGAL RESIDENCY, TO INHERIT, AND TO BE EQUAL IN THE EYES OF THE LAW.

Official Lesbian & Gay Solutions

BUT ONLY THOSE ABLE OR WILLING TO GET MARRIED. WE NEED TO FIGHT FOR BETTER HEALTHCARE, IMMIGRATION LAWS, LEGAL BENEFITS, AND FAMILY RECOGNITION FOR ALL!

Other Queer Approaches

DEAN SPADE

POLYNORMATIVITY AND KINKNORMATIVITY

Open non-monogamies have been suggested as potentially queerer and more ethical ways of relating than marriage/monogamy. However, Eleanor Wilkinson and Mimi Schippers have written about polynormativity in such relationships. Robin Bauer and Pepper Mint have made similar points about *kinknormativity* in BDSM.

Sexual acts being *transgressive* (of heteronormativity) doesn't necessarily mean they are *transformative*. Although kink practices do enable some people to resist heteronormativity and increase their awareness of cultural power dynamics, Elisabeth Sheff and Corie Hammers have also highlighted the race and class privilege present in many polyamorous and kink communities.

There's interest in "queer kinship" and the non-normative relationship, family, and community forms that are developing in queer contexts, such as relationship anarchy and solo-poly models.

IT AIN'T WHAT YOU DO, IT'S THE WAY THAT YOU DO IT.

We've seen that it has been just as important - if not more so - for queer theory to trouble the natural, taken-for-granted, and even coercive status of heterosexuality, as it is to study marginalized sexualities and genders. This leads to a question that often comes up in queer spaces:

If queer is something you do, rather than something you are, then surely the answer is yes. It's possible to be heterosexually attracted/relating without insisting that that is the natural or normal way of being, or that gender or sexuality are binary.

As authors such as Lynne Segal and Calvin Thomas have pointed out, it's also possible that some hetero attractions, practices, and relations will queer, or subvert, stable ideas of sexuality and gender as the assumed foundations of identities and relationships.

ANOTHER FUNNY TURN

In the early 2000s an influential *antisocial turn* took place, shifting away from projects that focused on reclaiming, reconstructing, and redeeming queer sex, sexuality, and gender, towards highlighting or embracing their antisocial or "negative" features.

Authors such as Leo Bersani, Lee Edelman, Lauren Berlant, Jack Halberstam, and Sara Ahmed have pointed out that heteronormativity is intrinsically linked with neoliberal, capitalist notions of what makes a "successful" self: being productive, reproductive, forward-looking, upwardly-mobile, and wealth-accumulating; and striving towards happiness, consumption, and stability in the form of "the good life". The temptation for queers to buy into these things can be seen as an assimilationist move. Hence Halberstam's focus on *the queer art of failure* as a form of creative engagement with the world, rather than an inability to comply with social norms.

NO FUTURE

Instead of trying to drag queerness into recognition by the queer liberalism approach of showing how productive, stable, and happy queers can be, antisocial queer theorists advocate adopting a deliberately antisocial stance. Instead of claiming gay pride we should celebrate queer shame.

In his book *No Future* (2004), Lee Edelman argues that queers have often been seen as threats to the kind of immortality and continuity that having offspring seems to offer. Instead of proving that queers can reproduce too, perhaps they should stand against such *cruel optimism*, as Lauren Berlant calls it, pointing out all of our inevitable mortality, and highlighting the problems underlying such neoliberal projects of hope: for example, ignoring the ecological implications of having kids.

QUEER FEELINGS

In her cultural critique *The Promise of Happiness* (2010), Sara Ahmed writes about the ways in which happiness – as it's currently constructed – is far more available to some than others, often those who can more easily conform to the "norm". She argues that happiness is a cultural imperative that directs us towards certain life choices and away from others. Happiness is promised to those who are willing to live their lives in the "right" way, e.g. marriage, kids, home, career.

Ahmed suggests that we require "unhappy queers", "feminist killjoys", and "melancholic migrants" to challenge this if we are to reach a more equal society where pleasure isn't always found at the expense of others or through conformity to problematic power hierarchies.

AFFECTIVE AND TEMPORALITY TURNS

Along with Sedgwick, Ahmed and Berlant are part of an *affective* turn in queer theory, turning their attention to emotional experience and the ways in which we affect and are affected by others, through feeling.

Other examples include Ann Cvetkovich's writing on depression as a cultural and political phenomenon, and Lyndsey Moon's research on how heterosexual therapists construct their clients' emotions. Queer clients are described as aggressive, frightened, venomous, and shameful; straight clients as assertive, proud, isolated, and vulnerable.

This has also involved a turn towards considering queer *temporality* (or time), with an emphasis on:

- *Futurity* (e.g. Muñoz's work on queer imagined futures)
- *Hauntology* (how the past and visions of the future haunt the present)
- *Queer (nonlinear) time* (e.g. an older trans person feeling younger than a younger trans person, in terms of years since transition)

QUEER TIME REFERS TO THE POTENTIALITY OF A LIFE UNSCRIPTED BY THE CONVENTIONS OF FAMILY, INHERITANCE, AND CHILD REARING.

Jack Halberstam

QUEER SUBJECTIVITY

In response to some of the criticisms of queer theory, many "antisocial" queer thinkers pay more attention to material realties and to national and transnational economic and political contexts.

Some have also turned more explicitly to lived experience and queer subjectivities. Ahmed brings together queer theory and phenomenology (the study of experience), and Muñoz suggests that queer writers draw on personal experiences.

Katherine Johnson proposes a *"psychosocial manifesto"* for studying sexuality. This brings together queer theoretical perspectives and the study of affective experience. For example, she analyses queer ambivalence (how queers can both desire belonging and acceptance, and reject the normativity that alienates them). She also explores how *affective activism* can offer possibilities for connection and transformation in the form of photographic exhibitions about queer experiences of suicidal feelings.

QUEER BEYOND QUEER

There are many burgeoning areas engaging with challenges around intersectionality. These either extend queer theory to particular intersections with sexuality and/or offer something back to queer theoretical considerations of these intersections.

Crip theory draws on social models of disability that locate disability in a society organized only around certain bodies (e.g. those that can climb stairs). Crip theory challenges discourses that limit bodies and pleasures to a normative/deviant binary, and also troubles the independent/dependent binary by pointing out how all bodies are *interdependent*, such as in relation to food and transport. Robert McRuer works in this area, and Helen Spandler writes in relation to madness and disablement.

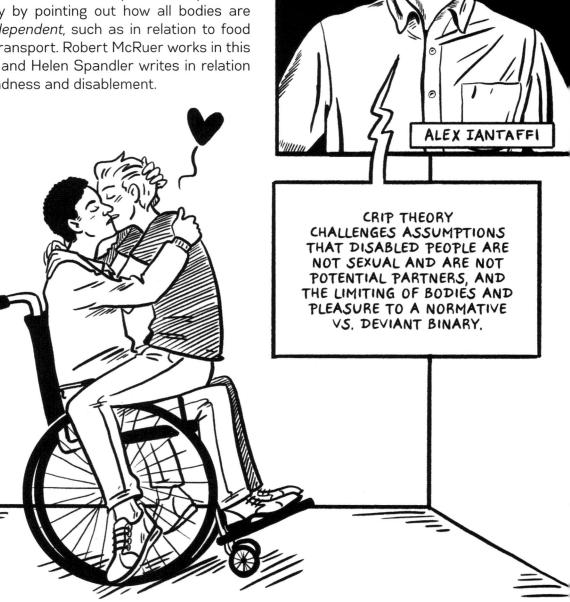

ALEX IANTAFFI

CRIP THEORY CHALLENGES ASSUMPTIONS THAT DISABLED PEOPLE ARE NOT SEXUAL AND ARE NOT POTENTIAL PARTNERS, AND THE LIMITING OF BODIES AND PLEASURE TO A NORMATIVE VS. DEVIANT BINARY.

ONE STEP BEYOND

Fat studies reframes the moral panic about "obesity" around the cultural production of fatphobia rather than fat bodies themselves. Authors such as Charlotte Cooper and Caroline Walters examine how fatness is involved in dominant discourses around gender, sexuality, race, class, etc.

Asexuality studies focuses on asexual experience and troubles the sexual imperative as a key aspect of heteronormativity, which takes for granted that it's natural and normal to experience sexual attraction. (Mark Carrigan, CJ Chasin, and Joseph De Lappe are a few key researchers in this field.)

Queer sex work draws together queer theory and sex work activism to trouble the heteronormative logics in play around sex work, to question binaries around work/not work, and again to contest the normative/deviant binary applied to sex workers' bodies. (Mary Laing and Allan Tyler are two contributors in this area.)

POST-QUEER?

People have argued that we're post-queer theory right from the start of this undisciplined discipline. This has happened even more since queer theory "came of age", with books and journals asking *What's Queer about Queer Studies Now?* (2005) and examining a *Post-Queer Politics* (2009), which would refocus from the heteronormative/queer boundary towards more intersectional understandings.

In *After Sex* (2011) a number of queer theorists address the question of what is not-queer about their writing, while also questioning what we even mean by "queer". And "sex". And "writing". And the concept of linear time that makes it possible to ask if we are "after" or "post" anything!

One major problem with the idea that we're post-queer theory is that so few of its key ideas and questions have filtered into everyday life. Queer theory still has a major task: of communicating its ideas to the people and places that matter.

OF PEOPLE ID AS **LGBT**

AROUND 5%

AROUND 80%

HAVE SOME KIND OF NON-NORMATIVE sexuality / gender / relationship

PEOPLE WITH SOME KINKY FANTASIES, PEOPLE WHO DON'T COMPLETELY FIT THE BINARY GENDER OR SEXUALITY BOXES...

QUEER COMMUNITIES

Queer theory has a lot to offer to queer, and other, communities in relation to common tensions that play out in their online and offline spaces.

We see this in the understandable desires to create:

- *Safe spaces* where only people with the same experiences or identities are included.
- Rules for appropriate/inappropriate behaviour within spaces (e.g. the importance of providing *trigger warnings* around some topics but not others, or adopting *non-violent communication* vs. avoiding *tone policing*).
- Norms of *calling out* bad behaviour through public shaming.
- Compensation for oppression by determining who has most right to speak.

NO STRAIGHTS

NO CIS GAYS

NO BIS

ONLY PEOPLE WHO LOOK QUEER ENOUGH

SUCH COMMUNITIES TEND TO CONTINUE TO CREATE HIERARCHIES WHERE CERTAIN GENDERED AND SEXUAL BODIES, IDENTITIES, AND BEHAVIOURS ARE DEEMED MORE LEGITIMATE THAN OTHERS.

JULIA SERANO

QUEERING COMMUNITIES

The risks of such community approaches include:

- The creation and policing of further hierarchical binaries and charmed circles/outer limits.
- Individualizing problematic behaviours rather than locating them within wider cultural discourses.
- Further exclusions (often related to class, age, culture, and disability) around the necessary levels of education and familiarity with terminologies required for inclusion.
- The pain of betrayal and shame that often results for people on "both sides" of an exclusion, on top of the bruising and battering already experienced as a result of wider cultural oppressions.
- Defaulting back to fixed identity as a reasonable basis for inclusion/exclusion and all the problems inherent in that.
- Dehumanizing and objectifying the excluded.
- Foregrounding certain identities over others in defining any community space (which we've seen is problematic throughout this book).

QUEER WAYS THROUGH THE DOUBLE BINDS?

Serano and others have argued that we therefore need to critically interrogate and resist the (normative) processes by which we default to "them and us" thinking and the double-binds these place people in. For example, the precarious position of insider who is terrified of "getting something wrong" versus the shameful position of outsider who has failed.

Importantly, this does not mean *discarding* the idea of safe(r) spaces; guidelines for ethical behaviour; or naming problematic actions, dynamics, or structural oppressions that are in play. That would involve swinging to the other side of yet another good/bad binary. Rather, it means recognizing the risks of building communities on essential notions of identity, universal assumptions, or them-and-us binaries.

THINKING QUEERLY

Our aim with this book is to be useful to people in their everyday lives, as well as introducing the academic world of queer theory. So, what might we pull out of queer theory if we wanted to start thinking and acting more queerly on an everyday basis?*

Try to avoid essentializing and unifying. Whatever you are considering is probably plural, rather than singular, and in process, rather than fixed and immutable. Can you discuss it in ways that reflect this diversity and fluidity? Can you simultaneously hold the multiple readings that are possible?

* You might try thinking through each of these suggestions in relation to a particular sexual or gender identity, practice, or representation. E.g. the last TV programme you watched, or conversation you had, on these matters.

THINKING (COMPLETELY) QUEERLY

Try to avoid polarizing into either/or binaries: male/female and straight/gay, but also, beyond that, (sex) positive/negative, good/bad, real/fake, essential/constructed, healthy/harmful, transgressive/conforming, assimilationist/liberatory, reformist/radical…

Instead ask what an idea or representation opens up and closes down. What is included and what is excluded? Might it be a matter of both/and rather than either/or?*

Remember queer = doing, not being. Focus on *how* something might be done queerly, rather than *what* is/isn't queer. Focus on what it *does* – what effects it has and what actions it achieves – rather than whether you think it's true/false or right/wrong.

* Of course it may be that it closes down a lot more than it opens up, or vice versa. Such an approach does not mean being uncritical, or ignoring ethical implications.

Subject all forms of sexuality and sexual representations to critical thinking and interrogation about the ideologies and power relations that they uphold (not just the obviously queer or transgressive ones, and not just the apparently straight or normative ones!).

Try to avoid the inevitable pull of individualism: locating issues in the individual person rather than circulating cultural discourses and structural processes. Try too to avoid the inevitable pull of identities, such as trying to define who does and doesn't belong, and who is queer and who isn't, and other thinking that creates "us and them" categories. Try to avoid universalizing: that all people on the inside/outside will share the same experiences.

Take heed of gender theorist Rosalind Gill's message. As queer theory has pointed out, the culture around us is highly binary, individualistic, essentialist, identity-based, and universalizing. There's a reason queer communities and theorists so often fall into the problematic thinking we've challenged here. It can be pretty unhelpful (not to mention individualizing) to beat yourself (or others) up each time you do this. Lisa Duggan suggests that queer is a radical potentiality that is sometimes realized and sometimes not.

Returning to the multiple definitions of "queer" we gave at the start of this book, let's aim to queer things through revealing the strangeness of normativity, disrupting the status quo, (re)claiming what is usually rejected, and forming new umbrella-alliances.

RESOURCES

We've mentioned as many key authors and books throughout this introduction as possible. Bear in mind that **speech bubbles attributed to these authors should not be read as direct quotes** - they're often paraphrased to give a sense of that author's ideas, rather than their exact words.

More detailed introductions to queer theory:

Sullivan, N. (2003). *A Critical Introduction to Queer Theory*. New York: New York University Press.
Spargo, T. (1999). *Foucault and Queer Theory*. London: Icon Books.
Wilchins, R.A. (2004). *Queer Theory, Gender Theory: An Instant Primer*. New York: Alyson Publications Inc.
Jagose, A. (1997). *Queer Theory: An Introduction*. New York: New York University Press.
Piontek, T. (2006). *Queering Gay and Lesbian Studies*. Champaign: University of Illinois Press.
Downing, L. (2008). *The Cambridge Introduction to Michel Foucault*. Cambridge: Cambridge University Press.

Accessible books on sexuality and gender:

Johnson, K. (2015). *Sexuality: A Psychosocial Manifesto*. Cambridge: Polity Press.
Weeks, J. (2009). *Sexuality*. London: Routledge.
Fausto-Sterling, A. (2012). *Sex/Gender: Biology in a Social World*. London: Routledge.
Fine, C. (2012). *Delusions of Gender*. London: Icon Books.
Richards, C. & Barker, M. (Eds.) (2013). *Sexuality and Gender for Mental Health Professionals: A Practical Guide*. London: Sage.
Jackson, S. & Scott, S. (2010). *Theorizing Sexuality*. Maidenhead: Open University Press.
Gauntlett, D. (2008). *Media, Gender and Identity: An Introduction*. London: Routledge.
Gill, R. (2006). *Gender and the Media*. London: Polity Press.

Edited collections on queer theory:

Hall, D.E. & Jagose, A. (Eds.) (2012). *The Routledge Queer Studies Reader*. London: Routledge.
Morland, I. & Willox, A. (Eds.) (2004). *Queer Theory*. Basingstoke: Palgrave Macmillan.
Richardson, D. & McLaughlin, J. (2012). *Intersections between Feminist and Queer Theory*. Basingstoke: Palgrave Macmillan.

Books on applied queer theory:

Serano, J. (2013). *Excluded: Making Feminist and Queer Movements More Inclusive*. New York: Seal Press.
Eisner, S. (2013). *Bi: Notes for a Bisexual Revolution*. New York: Seal Press.
Barker, M. (2013). *Rewriting the Rules: An Integrative Guide to Love, Sex and Relationships*. London: Routledge.
Bornstein, K. (2013). *My Gender Workbook*. London: Routledge.

Online resources:

Hey Hetero art project, http://tinafiveash.com.au/hey_hetero.html
Rochlin heterosexuality questionnaire, http://www.pinkpractice.co.uk/quaire.htm
Homoworld, http://www.youtube.com/watch?v=HJXw8PthDOM
Shields, K.R. & Tilmman, D., "Love Is All You Need?", http://loveisallyouneedthemovie.com/the-short
Bic pen reviews, http://thoughtcatalog.com/nico-lang/2013/02/the-10-best-amazon-reviews-of-bic-pens-for-her-so-far
Gender-switched parody of "Blurred Lines", https://www.youtube.com/watch?v=tKfwCjgiodg

ACKNOWLEDGEMENTS

Meg-John would like to thank Kiera Jamison, Hannah Darvill, Justin Hancock, Helen Bowes-Catton, Jay Stewart, Caroline Walters, Lisa Downing, Ed Lord, and Barney for inspiring them to write this book, and for helping with the writing.

Julia would like to thank Kiera Jamison and Meg-John Barker for making the experience of making this book both exciting and fun, and Alistair Bohm for help with the layout and countless cups of tea.

BIOGRAPHIES

Dr Meg-John Barker is a writer, therapist, and activist-academic, specializing in sexuality, gender, and relationship diversity. Meg-John is a senior lecturer in psychology at the Open University, co-founder of the *Psychology & Sexuality* journal, co-author of "The Bisexuality Report", and co-organizer of the Critical Sexology seminar series. Their main project is the creation of critical and kind self-help, including the books: *Rewriting the Rules, The Secrets of Enduring Love*, and *Enjoy Sex (How, When and If You Want To)*. They blog on www.rewriting-the-rules.com (including many posts and zines about queer issues like "What's wrong with heteronormativity", "Will gay rights and feminist movements please return to your assumptions", "Queer relationships", and "Privilege & Oppression, Conflict & Compassion").
Twitter: @megjohnbarker.

Julia Scheele is a freelance illustrator and graphic scribe, as well as a comics artist who has been active in the UK comics scene since 2008. Past clients include VICE Magazine, The Guardian, BBC4, Red Bull, Alain de Botton's The School Of Life, IBM, Edelman UK, Damn Fine Media, Scriberia and Kerrang!, amongst others, and her work has been featured in The Guardian, VICE UK, Dazed Digital and Digital Arts. She worked on the Image series *Phonogram: The Singles Club* by Kieron Gillen and Jamie McKelvie as an art assistant and is currently working as an artist on the series *Metroland*, written by Ricky Miller and published by Avery Hill Publishing. Apart from that, she runs the feminist zine collective One Beat Zines together with Sarah Broadhurst, with whom she produces regular anthologies themed around feminism and gender and also runs talks and workshops.
Online portfolio: www.juliascheele.co.uk
Twitter/Instagram: @juliascheele

Also available from Icon Books

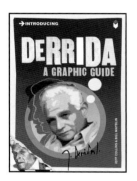  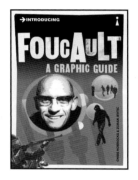 

introducingbooks.com